ARSENAL MATCH OF MY LIFE

ARSENAL MATCH OF MY LIFE

ALEX CROOK & PAT SYMES

FOREWORD BY
GEORGE GRAHAM

First published by Pitch Publishing, 2020

Pitch Publishing
A2 Yeoman Gate
Yeoman Way
Worthing
Sussex
BN13 3QZ
www.pitchpublishing.co.uk
info@pitchpublishing.co.uk

© 2020, Alex Crook & Pat Symes

Every effort has been made to trace the copyright.
Any oversight will be rectified in future editions at the
earliest opportunity by the publisher.

All rights reserved. No part of this book may be reproduced,
sold or utilised in any form or transmitted in any form or by
any means, electronic or mechanical, including photocopying,
recording or by any information storage and retrieval system,
without prior permission in writing from the Publisher.

A CIP catalogue record is available for this book
from the British Library.

ISBN 978 1 78531 311 0

Typesetting and origination by Pitch Publishing

Contents

Acknowledgements	7
Foreword	9
Theo Walcott: Arsenal 4-0 Aston Villa	17
Andrey Arshavin: Liverpool 4-4 Arsenal	27
Pat Rice: Arsenal 2-1 Leicester	37
David Seaman: Arsenal 1-0 Sheffield United	47
Alan Smith: Arsenal 1-0 Parma	59
Frank McLintock: Tottenham 0-1 Arsenal	71
Lee Dixon: Liverpool 0-2 Arsenal	81
Charlie Nicholas: Tottenham 2-4 Arsenal	91
Charlie George: Manchester City 1-2 Arsenal	105
Nigel Winterburn: Manchester United 0-1 Arsenal	113
Ray Parlour: Manchester United 0-1 Arsenal	125
Peter Marinello: Manchester United 2-1 Arsenal	137
Malcolm Macdonald: Arsenal 5-3 Newcastle United	147
David O'Leary: Juventus 0-1 Arsenal	155
Perry Groves: Arsenal 2-1 Liverpool	163
Paul Davis: Tottenham 1-2 Arsenal	173
Bob Wilson: Arsenal 3-0 Anderlecht	185
Anders Limpar: Arsenal 6-1 Coventry	193
John Jensen: Arsenal 1-3 Queens Park Rangers	201
Kevin Campbell: Arsenal 2-1 Sheffield Wednesday	211
Bobby Gould: Arsenal 1-3 Swindon	219
Sammy Nelson: Arsenal 3-2 Manchester United	227
Peter Storey: Arsenal 2-2 Stoke City	237
Piers Morgan	249

Acknowledgements

The authors would like to thank the following for their help in the preparation of this book: Adrian Clarke, Alex Montgomery, Will Price, Adrian Durham, Jim White, Rob Knox, Jake Rusby, Mark Bullen, Connor Armstrong, Sam Matterface, Neil Allen, Joe Batchelor, Mike White and Jean Bernard Le Fur.

Also, a special mention to Alex's wife Emma for giving him the inspiration for the project with her love for Arsenal and of course to the cast list of Gunners greats who so willingly gave up their time to share their special stories with us.

Foreword

Anyone lucky enough to have represented Arsenal will only have good things to say about their experiences, so to be able to proclaim I won trophies with them as both a player and a manager is something that I am immensely proud of.

It is one of the biggest clubs in the world and some of the most famous names in the game have pulled on the famous red-and-white jersey. It is also the club that is most special to me and the one that gave me the greatest memories from a football career I absolutely loved.

I was an okay player but nothing special by Arsenal's standards, especially in later years when some of the players they had were truly world class. I was up and down; there were some games where I was good but a lot of games where I was the opposite. Luckily enough, we did manage to win things while I was there as a player, thanks largely to my talented team-mates.

I'd had a good couple of seasons at Chelsea when Tommy Docherty decided to break up our young team and I was one of the players sold in the summer of 1966, making the move from west to north London. Full-back Bob McNab joined Arsenal at the same time and they were trying to rebuild the team under Bertie Mee.

Bertie was a brilliant organiser and managed the whole footballing side of the club from the youth team to the reserves, all the way up to the first team, but he was not a coach who was on the training pitch every day and left that to Dave Sexton and, latterly, Don Howe.

I played under Dave when he was a coach at Chelsea so I knew how good he was and, when he left to go back to Stamford Bridge, Don came in. They were two brilliant coaches who definitely rubbed off on me so I learned an awful lot from them both.

We had some great characters in our team like Charlie George, who was very opinionated and had strong views about the game. He is still the same to this day. He just had outstanding natural talent and nobody could tell him what to do because Charlie knew what he wanted to do when he was on the pitch. He was great going forward and was also a local boy, born just up the road from Highbury, so was a big Arsenal fan as well. He also loved the media because he was very talkative.

Alongside Charlie there was Frank McLintock, who to me is one of Arsenal's true greats. He was the inspiration in the team for a number of years and was a terrific captain. When you went to places like Anfield or Old Trafford you would look over your shoulder and see Frank there and it was like having three players rolled into one.

I felt sorry for Frank because he kept getting to cup finals and losing them, four in a row as I recall, so there was a stage when he thought he would never win one. I knew we were on the right path, but when we finally beat Anderlecht over two legs to lift the 1970 Inter-Cities Fairs Cup, it was an unbelievable feeling.

Bob Wilson was also part of that team and he was a fantastic goalkeeper and later a coach at Arsenal as well. Bob and I made our Scotland debuts in the same game alongside Kenny Dalglish and the two of us travelled up to Glasgow together. The rest of the players could not understand Bob's English accent and it was a bit strange to have an Englishman playing in goal for Scotland.

The Fairs Cup victory was the start of a good spell of success for the club, and we went on to win the League and FA Cup Double in 1971. I thought I had scored in the cup final against Liverpool at Wembley because the ball was bobbling around in the box and I was sure I got a touch to put it into the net. All of my team-mates congratulated me and were saying things like, 'Well done George, you have won the cup.' It was a great moment until after the game when Jimmy Hill announced on television that I did not get a touch and the goal was taken away from me and given to Eddie Kelly, which I am still not entirely convinced about, but at least we won.

I wish I could have brought Arsenal more success as a player and it was something that really got under my skin once I became manager: trying to put them back on the winning trail again.

As a youth coach at both Crystal Palace and Queens Park Rangers, I worked quite a lot with Terry Venables and learned an awful lot from him in terms of how he set up a team to play in a certain system.

That type of learning was invaluable for me so, when I became a manager, I knew exactly how we were going to play and it was just a matter of getting the players to function the way I wanted them to. I also knew the type of player I wanted to sign and used to buy the regional sports newspapers from all around the country every week, papers like the *Sports Argus* in Birmingham, the Sheffield *Green 'Un* and the Newcastle *Chronicle*.

I felt that gave me an edge over other managers because it helped me form an opinion of who was playing well for their club. I remember reading that Lee Dixon had won Stoke City's Player of the Year three years on the trot so I thought he must be a good player. I went to watch him a few times and saw Steve Bould playing alongside him, so I signed the pair of them.

I wanted to build a team with stability at the back so, as well as Dixon and Bould, I got Nigel Winterburn from Wimbledon to replace the great Kenny Sansom at left-back. I recruited some unfancied players like Kevin Richardson from Watford and I could also call upon one of the best youth policies in the country thanks to, among others, Pat Rice.

When I was appointed, we had about eight outstanding young players all ready to come into the first team, including David Rocastle, Paul Davis, Michael Thomas, Tony Adams and Martin Keown – I could virtually name a whole team of them. I had seen Tony play when I was managing the youth team at QPR and by the time I arrived at Arsenal he was not only ready to play but was virtually ready to be captain because he was such a fantastic leader on and off the pitch. Rocastle was an outstanding talent, unbelievable, and it was a very hard decision to sell Rocky to Leeds in 1992 but he had picked up a knee injury and we were told it was so bad that he could not play more than one game a week. It was unfortunate but, to be a top team challenging for trophies, you are going to have to play more than just once a week. Rocky was still outstanding in the matches he did play and without the injury he would have been an England regular.

That blend of youth and the experienced players I had signed from the lower division was a fantastic combination and came together very nicely and also a lot more quickly than I expected. The beauty of it was they were all like young students, hungry for information and guidance, and I pushed them, probably too hard at times, but it paid off because one minute I was buying lower division players and promoting youngsters and not long afterwards they were winning championships.

Another very shrewd purchase I made was bringing in David Seaman to replace John Lukic as goalkeeper. John had turned down the offer of a new contract so I knew I would have problems with him, but I think he had a bit of a shock when David arrived.

From the moment I met him, I knew David had great enthusiasm and a passion for the game and that is what I always looked for in my players. Before making any signing, I would try and find out from other coaches and managers how good the player was in training and how good he was off the pitch. I would ask: 'Is he ambitious? Does he want to win things?'

FOREWORD

You have to do background checks when you are a manager and we did not have a massive scouting department back in those days.

Alan Smith was another great signing and does not get the credit he deserves for scoring goals that were important to our successes including when we snatched the league at Anfield in 1989 and the winner in the final of the European Cup Winners' Cup against Parma. He won the Golden Boot for two years running but never got the publicity and adulation of some of his team-mates.

The title win in 89 is undoubtedly the greatest moment of my career and Lee Dixon tells the story about how I told the players we would be drawing 0-0 at half-time and go on to get the 2-0 victory we needed to overhaul Liverpool at the top. That is not true, as I actually said we would win 3-0!

Liverpool were all-conquering at that time so I decided to play with three central defenders. We had done the same thing against Manchester United at Old Trafford earlier in the season and came away with a 1-1 draw after Tony Adams had scored at both ends.

We got a lot of stick at the time because people felt the system was too defensive, but they did not understand how much the full-backs would push on. I always planned to play that way at Anfield and seeing that plan come together in such dramatic circumstances was an unbelievable feeling, something you dream of.

Nick Hornby wrote a book about it called *Fever Pitch* that was later turned into a popular film. I love watching that, especially the scene where the main character, a schoolteacher and long-suffering Arsenal fan, gets his schoolkids to all stand in a line during a match with their hands in the air trying to replicate our famous offside trap. The film also compares me to a schoolteacher methodically planning lessons, which I take as a big compliment.

Beating Parma in the European final was another huge achievement because they were a phenomenal team, one of the best in Italy at that time. It was fitting we won that cup with a 1-0 scoreline as that was what the Arsenal fans used to sing, but I did not just want to win 1-0, I wanted more – I wanted to win 3-0 every week.

I was often asked why we did not play more adventurously but, like Bertie, I knew how I wanted the team to be organised and I was never swayed away from that. It worked for us for seven or eight years and we did well and won things. I also think the quality of the two goals we scored at Anfield is often overlooked.

Obviously, when Arsene Wenger was appointed he was much more of an attacking manager and he brought in some unbelievable players from abroad for peanuts, players that nobody else in England had ever heard of. Arsene's buying early on was phenomenal when you think of Thierry Henry, Emmanuel Petit, Patrick Vieira and the like.

He brought these unpolished gems and made them into fantastic, world-class players and Arsenal should have probably won the Champions League with that team, because they were good enough.

I enjoyed watching Arsene's side play, especially the Invincibles – and that is my one regret, that my Arsenal team never managed to go a whole season unbeaten. We came close in the 1990/91 title-winning campaign when we only lost one game, a 2-1 defeat to Chelsea at Stamford Bridge, but that never really gets mentioned in the media.

It was during my time as Arsenal manager that the now-famous Tuesday club was formed and I must confess I never knew at the time the full extent of what my players were drinking during their midweek get togethers.

That simply could not happen any more as football has changed so much and modern players are athletes. It makes me

FOREWORD

grateful that I played when I did as I would not get anywhere near the squad now, let alone the starting line-up!

Anyway, I hope you enjoy reliving your favourite Arsenal moments as much as I did and I look forward to adding this book to the rest of my Gunners library.

George Graham
April 2020

THEO WALCOTT

Theo Walcott
Forward
2006–2018

Theo Walcott's rise to superstardom was as rapid as one of his 100m sprints. A product of Southampton's much-heralded youth academy, the Berkshire-raised speedster joined Arsenal for £5m in January 2006 aged just 16 and was a surprise inclusion in England's World Cup squad months later after becoming the Three Lions' youngest-ever senior international. A member of the Gunners' 100 Club, despite not being recognised as an out and out striker, Walcott was part of the side Arsene Wenger led to FA Cup glory in 2015 and again two years later. He is also the only player in the club's history to score in both the League Cup and FA Cup finals, but it is that 2015 triumph over Aston Villa which he regards as the standout moment in his Arsenal career after fighting back from a serious knee injury to become a Wembley winner.

Arsenal 4-0 Aston Villa

FA Cup Final
Saturday, 30 May 2015
Wembley, London
Attendance: 89,283

Arsenal	Aston Villa
Szczesny	Given
Bellerin	Hutton
Mertesacker	Okore
Koscielny	Vlaar
Monreal	Richardson (Bacuna)
Coquelin	Cleverley
Cazorla	Westwood (Sanchez)
Ramsey	Delph
Ozil (Wilshere)	N'Zogbia (Agbonlahor)
Sanchez (Oxlade-Chamberlain)	Benteke
Walcott (Giroud)	Grealish

Managers

Arsene Wenger   Tim Sherwood

Goals

Walcott
Sanchez
Mertesacker
Giroud

'Theo, are you sitting down?' I still remember the words of the Arsenal club doctor that followed that made me break down in front of my wife, Mel. That is when the enormity of my knee injury hit me, the moment I knew I would be facing a year without being able to play the game I loved.

I had actually suffered the injury during our FA Cup third-round win over Tottenham the season before the match of my Arsenal life. It was a weird one because, even as I was being carried off on a stretcher, sat upright and famously gesturing the 2-0 scoreline to the baying Spurs fans, it did not feel like the injury was as serious as it turned out to be. I did not have any swelling either so surely that had to be a sign the damage was not too bad? How wrong I was.

After hearing the grim assessment during that fateful telephone call I could not bring myself to go into the training ground because I did not want the rest of the players to see me when I was feeling weak. It was a tough journey, but eventually the physio got me going again and I managed to find the strength to face my team-mates and quickly realised they loved me being around, which spurred me on even more to get back to full fitness.

It was a horrible time in my 12-year Arsenal career, one which gave me so many great moments and fantastic memories. It is also the reason that none of the 108 goals I scored is more treasured than the one which set us on the way to making FA Cup history.

You can score hat-tricks against Newcastle or get big goals in the Champions League, but our emphatic Wembley win over Aston Villa meant so much because it came at the end of a long, agonising road to recovery.

After such a serious lay-off it was a flip of a coin between Olivier Giroud and me as to who was going to play at Wembley. Olivier played most of the season and had done really well, whereas I had only had little bits of games because I was easing my way back in.

We played West Brom a week before the final and I started up front and scored a hat-trick after which I felt like the manager could not leave me out, although it was only a few hours before kick-off that I knew for sure I was definitely starting.

Some managers like to tell you the team earlier so everyone has it in their heads and can work on tactics but Arsene Wenger used to want everybody to prepare as if they were starting so kept us all on our toes as long as possible.

We stayed in the Hilton Hotel overlooking Wembley the night before the final and I was able to stand on the balcony of my room and look down at all the fans excitedly making their way to the stadium, which I loved. People have suggested the magic of the FA Cup has been diluted since the advent of the Premier League but, for me, as an English player, I am proud to be able to say I have lifted the famous trophy.

In beating Villa, we also set a new record of the most FA Cup wins by a single team of 12, which became 13 when we defeated Chelsea two years later. To be part of that history is something that can never be taken away and to be able to say I scored the opening goal makes it even more special.

It was a decent goal as well and started when Francis Coquelin played a long diagonal ball down the left-hand side for me to have a run at Villa right-back Alan Hutton. I spotted that our left-back Nacho Monreal had made an overlapping run so passed it on for him to cross into the area on to the head of Alex Sanchez. Alexis has an unbelievable spring for someone of his size, helped by the fact he used to train wearing ankle weights, which I tried once before deciding it was not for me. He sprung and headed the ball back and just as Santi Cazorla was about to shoot, I came from nowhere and smashed the ball in at the near post with my left foot.

You could see all the emotion come out in my celebration because it meant so much to me after being injured for so long. It was even more magical because all of my family who had supported me so much were sat in that corner of the stadium, which meant I could share the moment with them.

My son Finley was there and it was nice the morning after the game to see him walking around the team hotel with the FA Cup. After the previous year's final, I took a picture of Finley inside the cup with Arsene alongside, which would have been a great family snap but for the fact my toddler was crying his eyes out.

We dominated the whole of the Villa game and could have been more than just one goal in front when Alexis Sanchez made it 2-0 early in the second half with an absolute rocket shot. He just got the ball out from under his feet quickly and before Shay Given knew anything about it, the Villa goalkeeper was picking it out of his net.

Alexis got so much movement on the shot, which we had seen him do countless times in training, and he was a player that even in five-a-side matches you wanted on your team because he was capable of doing some mad stuff. He just loved playing football and the coaching staff used to find it difficult to get him off the training pitch. Even the day before a game he would be doing 100 extra shots after training, but that is just the type of guy he was and it worked for him, at Arsenal anyway.

That goal was the signal for the floodgates to really open and soon we were 4-0 up and cruising thanks to a header from Per Mertesacker, our giant German defender, and a cheeky back heel from super sub Olivier Giroud.

Per arranged a lot of the post-match party and was the life and soul of it. Just picture a big seven-foot man up dancing and getting all the wives and girlfriends up on the floor with him and you will get the idea.

I was delighted for Olivier to come on and score having been left out of the starting line-up. After I got the hat-trick the week before he said to me, 'Sh*t, I am not playing am I?' and if the boot was on the other foot I would have thought exactly the same, but

Olivier was a great professional and never sulked in the dressing room before the game.

In all my time at Arsenal, Olivier and Robin van Persie were the two players I most loved playing with. They both held the ball up very well and were very elegant at times. Olivier will always do a job for the team even if he is not scoring, as we saw at the 2018 World Cup with France. If he was not playing, I don't think they would have been able to win that tournament.

Olivier had a good understanding with Mesut Ozil, who seems to get a lot of stick but I think that is mainly down to his demeanour and body language, but that is just the way he is even on a day-to-day basis. As a team-mate you are used to that and know he is not sulking as other people outside the club maybe surmise.

Cesc Fabregas was the best midfielder I played with because I would just make a run, not have to break stride and the ball would magically appear in front of me, thanks to his vision. Mesut was very similar in the way he made everything look so easy and like he was not even trying. He was also good at weighing up the strengths of his team-mates; for example, he knew that Olivier liked balls played into his feet whereas I loved having something to run on to. There are a lot of players with that ability but he has done it on a consistent basis for many years.

As I have already mentioned, we had a good night after the game and it was nice to see Arsene so relaxed at the party at our hotel and letting his hair down, not that he had much. It was good for him to see how much love we, as a group of players, all had for our manager.

Arsene is a man that always has a lot of time for people anyway, but on those particular evenings he would always join in with the celebrations – unless it came to dancing. I never ever saw him dance!

I actually convinced myself that night that he was going to leave, because there was a lot of emotion in him and when I spoke to him and his coaching staff it felt like a last supper-type scenario. He was just watching everyone enjoy themselves and taking it all in.

Deep down he must have thought, 'I can't leave this now', because he ended up staying another three years and winning another FA Cup.

I always felt like Arsene took a lot of unfair flack for a manager that had led the team into the Champions League season after season. Arsenal have been in a transition stage since he left and that proves it was no easy task to achieve what he did, so I feel like now people are starting to appreciate his job a lot more.

Arsene was great for developing the young players coming through, particularly in the cup competitions. He always gave us the opportunity to show what we could do and that is probably why he won so many FA Cups, because it was a great stage to perform on. I think he enjoyed watching these youngsters fulfil their potential and took a lot of satisfaction in seeing them reach their goal.

I was only 16 when I joined the club and that was a very strange time because it was done under a veil of secrecy. I had played for the Southampton first team but was still sharing a dressing room with the scholars and it was hard to lie to my mates about whether I was leaving or not.

On the day the move was going through I did not turn up for training and was getting loads of messages and phone calls, but could not tell them what was going on until it was officially announced.

That was in the January and I was called up for England's World Cup squad the following summer, which was a crazy time. I did not know I was going until my name came up on Sky Sports News and that was before I had even got the phone call from the FA.

My inclusion at such a young age created a lot of chatter on television and it was all way too much for me to take in. Even though it was exciting I was totally overwhelmed, so I ended up turning off the TV and playing World Cup-themed Monopoly with my dad. It was the longest Monopoly game ever!

Arsene had told me a few weeks earlier that Sven-Goran Eriksson, the England manager, was coming to watch me train but I did not think much of it at the time, so for him to select me was totally surreal.

I am sure nobody will disagree that Arsene also liked his teams to play football in an attractive way and that was a big draw for me when I signed: the pace and interchanges of players. At 16 you just think about playing with freedom and expressing yourself and do not look too much into tactics. I certainly didn't.

For me, even now, when I think of Arsenal, I think of Arsene and Thierry Henry.

Every kid playing football in the playground pretends to be their favourite player and I was always trying to imitate Thierry. I just wanted to be him so when I actually got to meet and play with him, I was like a starstruck little boy. I always remember the day I beat him in a sprint test and thought to myself, 'Wow. I am quicker than Thierry.' Again, it was a lot to take in but I remember from day one that Ashley Cole and Sol Campbell just grabbed me and put their arms around me and looked after me until they left the club. Having those two strong characters looking out for me in a dressing room full of players who had been Invincibles just a couple of seasons before helped me a lot.

Every day after training Thierry would grab Ashley for extra sprinting training. He would say: 'You know where I am going to go but I am going to knock the ball past you and will always get there before you.' He made it look so effortless and would just glide past players.

I used to try and do it myself to Ashley but physically I was not strong enough so he could brush me away, but it was great training against Ashley every day and seeing the way Thierry would try different ways to get past him. That stuck with me and eventually, when Ashley moved on, he and I enjoyed some great battles.

After Thierry left for Barcelona, I ended up taking his number 14 shirt but that was almost by accident as I wanted Ian Wright's old number eight jersey. Then we signed Samir Nasri and he took the number eight so I said: 'Okay, I will have 14.' It was only when our long-serving kit man Vic Akers pointed out that was Thierry's number that I realised, but I took it anyway.

One of my favourite mementos from my career is the shirt I wore when I scored my first goal for Arsenal in the 2007 League Cup Final against Chelsea. I got Thierry to sign it and he wrote something like, 'First of many but only 227 to go', because that is how many goals he scored.

Thierry was a great guy to have in the dressing room, very loud, and would always shout 'Lewis' at me as he used to say I looked like Lewis Hamilton.

Emmanuel Eboue was just as loud and it was a really good dressing room to learn and develop in. There were a lot of strong characters in there so at times I would just duck my head and get on with things. I always felt like Thierry wanted me to get more involved but at 16, 17 I did not really know how to interact with people in their primes.

I worked it out in the end and loved my time at Arsenal. As with any club I had some ups and downs but I worked with some fantastic people, both in terms of players and staff. The whole club itself was one massive family and as a family man that was perfect for me. Whenever I put on that red top it felt like home.

The football itself was great; making history at the Emirates, playing in front of those amazing fans under the lights on Champions League nights, scoring more than 100 goals and having my name alongside great players like Dennis Bergkamp and my hero Thierry. Nobody can take that away from me.

ANDREY ARSHAVIN

Andrey Arshavin
Forward
2009–2013

Andrey Arshavin was Arsenal's most expensive player at £15m when he joined the Gunners from his home city club of Zenit St Petersburg on transfer deadline day in January 2009, and over four profitable years scored 31 goals in 144 appearances as a striker and winger. Arshavin was 28 when he arrived in a snowstorm, which all but brought Heathrow Airport to a standstill, and by then had been named Russia's Player of the Year and figured prominently in his country's rise to the semi-finals of Euro 2008. Arshavin might be unique among ex-Arsenal players in having a degree in fashion design and has also written three books. In one of them he controversially questioned whether or not women should be allowed to drive. Arshavin, a fans' favourite at Arsenal, later returned to his former club and wound down his career with a year in the Kazakhstan Premier League. If for nothing else, he wrote himself a page in Arsenal history for one spectacular goalscoring feat at Liverpool. Naturally, the 4-4 draw at Liverpool, three months after moving to England, is the match of Arshavin's Arsenal life. 'From Russia with goals', said the headlines next day and how right they were.

Liverpool 4-4 Arsenal

Premier League
Tuesday, 21 April 2009
Anfield, Liverpool
Attendance: 44,424

Liverpool	**Arsenal**
Reina	Fabianski
Arbeloa	Sagna
Carragher	Toure
Agger	Silvestre
Aurelio	Gibbs
Alonso	Song
Mascherano	Fabregas
Benayoun	Denilson (Walcott)
Kuyt (Nabil)	Arshavin
Riera (Babel)	Nasri
Torres	Bendtner (Diaby)

Managers

Rafael Benitez Arsene Wenger

Goals

Torres (2) Arshavin (4)
Benayoun (2)

I do not think I spent more than half an hour with Arsene Wenger when he was trying to sign me in December 2008. He had spotted me at Euro 2008 and I flew over to the Emirates to speak to him. I told him I wasn't against the move and he told me where he saw me playing on the pitch. A month later I made the switch. The clubs didn't agree the fee – an Arsenal record at the time – until the very last minute. I can now reveal that the transfer did not actually take place until a couple of minutes after the January window had closed. It was a big upheaval for me but, as a Russian used to buckets of it, I was reassured by the sight of snow everywhere when I landed in England. No planes were flying between London and Paris and there were few cars on the roads into London. Those that had braved the terrible conditions were having trouble negotiating a straight line. Just like home. In fact, after being told it never snowed in London, it did so every winter I was there. We drove out of London, then to offices at the Emirates, and I didn't see much of my new home city for at least two weeks.

The weather may have been cold but the welcome I got at Arsenal was warm. I got on well with Arsene. 'The Professor', as I saw him, delved deeply into football and had his own philosophy about the way the game should be played. I had a fair working relationship with him and enjoyed listening to his ideas. He is an intellectual but not so dogmatic that he didn't listen to the views of others and he never forced his ideas on his players. He wanted us to think and to show that we were thinking. I compare him to Guus Hiddink and Dick Advocaat, two very experienced coaches who led the Russian national side, except that he was more reasonable than perhaps they were and maybe a little bit more old-fashioned; that may sound a little strange but that's what I felt about him. Arsene loved technical footballers and he loved us to attack, a fundamental belief not always shared by others, and I noted how very good he was at spotting a young talent before anyone else and bringing it through. What I liked about him was that he was always honest. He told me what he thought about me, my game and what I should be doing. All players like to know where they stand and Arsene was completely straight in his dealings with me.

Settling in a new city is never easy and most of the Arsenal players at the time were younger than me but they all tried to help with the language and other problems. The younger guys in particular explained key words. Luckily the Arsenal dressing room had a multitude of nationalities so that I was not alone and we quickly found a common language, a means of communication among local and foreign players. I never felt left out. I quickly became friends with quite a lot of players. At the start it was Cesc Fabregas, Samir Nasri and Tomas Rosicky, possibly because we lived near each other, so we were able to socialise. Nasri was living with Tatiana Golovin, a French woman with Russian roots, and we were particularly friendly with them. Later, I got on well with Lukas Podolski and Per Mertesacker, who were kind and considerate towards me, and me and my family went on holiday with Emmanuel Eboue and his family. Overall, I had no trouble mixing with the Arsenal players, even though there was always a big turnover.

For the first three months of my Arsenal career I lived outside London in a hotel near the training ground. I did almost nothing except go backwards and forwards from the hotel to the training ground. Occasionally my family and I met other Russians living in London to catch up with news from home and then later we found a home in London and settled in the best we could. I spent time with my children, took them to school and to extra classes and activities afterwards. We went out into the countryside to play polo with Russian friends, although I was mostly a spectator, and ventured to that most British of venues, the horse racing at Ascot. When the ATP tennis came to town, we used to go along and watch and of course lots of big stars had concerts in London. We had no trouble filling our time.

I made my debut against Sunderland in February and was gradually adjusting to my new club, my new team-mates, my new manager and my new life, when the fixture list came up with Liverpool away. I think it was my first big match and I realised just how much it meant to Arsenal fans. There was an evening kick-off and we were staying outside Liverpool in a hotel near a golf course. I prepared for the big occasion by watching Sky Sports all day since there was not much else to do and there was nothing about the build-up to suggest this match was going to be any different from those I had already played in. Nothing to indicate I was about to make a small piece of history.

In Russia, scoring four goals in a match is known as a 'poker'. This was my first poker and also my last but I will always remember it, four goals at the great Anfield stadium in front of all those famous fans. The Kop has the reputation for housing the very best supporters and they weren't used to opposition players coming to Liverpool and scoring so many in front of them. It was a magical evening and the only shame was that we didn't win. For me, scoring four goals at Liverpool was not at the time especially significant and only after I had accomplished my feat did I realise just how important it was in the context of English football. Anfield is such an iconic stadium, one of the oldest and steeped in history, and witness to so many big matches over the years. Only once had any opposition player had the temerity to score four goals in front of them, when Dennis Westcott of Wolverhampton Wanderers achieved the feat in 1946, a long time before I was born.

Looking back on it, I had four shots and scored four goals. It was that simple. In fact, the official statistics reveal that Liverpool had four shots and scored four times and the same with us. It was not as though shots and headers were coming in from all angles all evening. For me, it was a magical occasion when everything came together. When I got to my hat-trick in the 70th minute to make it 3-2, we were winning easily and on top; we should have found a way to hold on.

My first goal in the 36th minute was a shot which went in off the crossbar but Liverpool struck twice early in the second half through Fernando Torres and Yossi Benayoun. From being in a strong position at the break, we were suddenly behind. Then in the 67th minute I dispossessed Alvaro Arbeloa to score with a right-foot shot for the equaliser. My third came from ten yards and that should have been enough. Torres could do no wrong for Liverpool at that time and he made it 3-3 in the 72nd. As Liverpool pressed for a late winner, it looked like it would be us who were going to be the victors when, on a breakaway, I beat Pepe Reina, the Liverpool goalkeeper, with my left foot. Surely the match was over. But no, deep into time added on, a mistake in defence let in Benayoun for Liverpool's fourth. Soon afterwards, an extraordinary match was over and, despite my achievement, we had to be content with a point. Liverpool were top at the time but they did not go on and clinch the title. They may well have regretted only drawing with us at such a crucial time in the season.

What did Arsene say afterwards? I don't remember the exact words. I do remember his emotions; he was smiling and patted me on the back of my head. He had taken a chance in paying so much money for me and this was his justification. We all signed the match ball, as is customary, and it was presented to me as a keepsake. I have to say that many years on I don't know where that ball is, or even if it's still in existence. Back at the hotel, I didn't sleep much that night because I was mentally exhausted and still reliving every goal. Later they showed my goals on Channel One, Russia's main TV channel, which was nice and helped me realise exactly what I had managed to do. I think I also realised at that moment that scoring four goals in a match was never going to happen to me again. And so it proved. My only poker.

I went on to have four happy years at Arsenal but I am sorry we never won anything in my time there. Every year we seemed to sell our best players. Nasri, Fabregas and Robin van Persie, all big players for us, were all allowed to leave and their sale weakened the team without a doubt. This was unpleasant for me because I had come to Arsenal to win the title, and losing the 2011 League Cup Final to Birmingham, a team later to be relegated, was doubly disappointing. That was a huge shame, because I did not go to England for the money; I could have got the same at any number of clubs elsewhere. I wanted to at least win a trophy in England and to compete in the Champions League. Unfortunately, there were better teams than us and realistically – objectively speaking – the team we had at the time, constantly losing important players, was not capable of winning the big prizes.

Mikel Arteta was one of the players brought in while I was there. He came from Everton and quickly strengthened the team. At Everton he had been a wide midfielder but with us he was deployed in a more defensive role. He quickly became a team leader and Arsene made him captain. Before the game he always had something important to say and at half-time he always gave his opinions in a strong voice. Looking back, there were signs then that he might become a coach but I don't think Arteta himself would have thought in his wildest dreams that he would become Arsenal's manager so soon.

I hope Arsenal fans enjoyed my performances for them. They called me the 'Little Magician' and I was well received overall. If I met them on the streets, I could sense their support for me and I never had any problems with them. Maybe towards the end, a few complained about me in an emotional outburst or two. They wanted to win trophies as much as I did, so they might have been frustrated. But these were rare. When I come to London now, the fans recognise me and this helps me feel that in a way I was able to leave my mark on the history of the club. All any player can hope for is to give the supporters some pleasant memories and I think I did that – thanks to one extraordinary night in Liverpool in particular.

PAT RICE

Pat Rice
Defender
1967–1980
Assistant manager
1996–2012

Even Arsene Wenger described Belfast-born Pat Rice as an Arsenal legend and it is hard to disagree when the facts are examined. Raised in north London, Rice joined the Gunners as an apprentice in 1964 and, apart from three years at Watford at the tail end of his career, he spent some 44 years in the service of Arsenal as a player, academy boss, caretaker manager and finally as trusted and respected number two to Wenger through some of the greatest matches in the club's history. His remarkable litany of successes began with the FA Youth Cup in 1966 and was followed by the Football League title in 1971 and the FA Cups of 1971 and 1979. He was Arsenal's Player of the Year in 1972 and played in five FA Cup finals, one of only three players to do so. Returning to Arsenal from Watford, he was in charge of the academy when they won the FA Youth Cups of 1988 and 1994, producing some outstanding talent for Wenger and his predecessors. As assistant to the great Frenchman, Rice helped preside over three league titles, four FA Cup Final victories and three Community Shields. Briefly, for three matches, he was Arsenal's manager before the arrival of Wenger (none of them lost), before becoming adviser, confidante and an occasional shoulder to cry on for one of Arsenal's most revolutionary bosses. Rice retired in 2012, a job well done, and was awarded the MBE in the same year. Not least among the many shining achievements of the Wenger–Rice era came in 2003/04 when Arsenal went through the entire league season without losing (26 wins, 12 draws). The Arsenal team became known as the Invincibles and in fact extended their unbeaten run the following season to an incredible 49 league games. The Premier League title was won against Tottenham on 25 April – satisfying enough in itself – but to complete the 38-game season without defeat could only be accomplished on the last day of the season when modest Leicester visited Highbury.

Arsenal 2-1 Leicester

Premier League
Sunday, 15 May 2004
Highbury, London
Attendance: 38,419

Arsenal	Leicester
Lehmann	Walker (Coyne)
Lauren	Dabizas
Campbell	Heath
Toure	Sinclair
Cole	Stewart
Gilberto Silva	Freund (Brooker)
Vieira	McKinlay
Ljungberg (Keown)	Nalis
Pires (Edu 70)	Scowcroft
Bergkamp (Reyes)	Bent
Henry	Dickov (Benjamin)

Managers

Arsene Wenger   Micky Adams

Goals

Henry (pen)   Dickov
Vieira

To go through a whole league season without losing is an incredible achievement and possibly ours has been a little underestimated outside Arsenal. Who would have thought anyone could have beaten Liverpool in 2019/20, so brilliant was their football? It really didn't look as if anybody could touch them but struggling Watford did and 3-0 is a heavy defeat by any standards. In the present-day Premier League you can lose to anyone on any day if your standards drop just a little, as Liverpool's did that day at Vicarage Road, and in 2003/04 it was no different. There was always a potential nasty surprise around every corner. Our standards never dipped that year. We have been criticised in retrospect for drawing so many of our league fixtures, but that shows how determined we were not to lose even when not playing at our best. Some days you have to accept you are collectively as a team off the mark, as we were occasionally that season. Everyone has good and bad days. The next best thing in that situation was to make sure we didn't lose. Just as the team left the dressing room to go out on to the pitch, we used to say to the players: 'Hey, we are hard to beat today.' We didn't aim to draw so often but we turned it into an art, the art of not being beaten under any circumstances. The favourite old chant of 'One-nil to the Arsenal' restarted around this time and we were quite proud of it.

I have a tape of the whole season which I have never looked at. But I can easily enough remember some great players and some outstanding matches.

The summer leading up to it, we were not especially busy in the transfer market. We brought in Jens Lehmann in goal after letting David Seaman wind down his great career at Manchester City, but otherwise Arsene was keen to promote from within, via the academy system. Arsene liked players who understood what Arsenal were about, for whom the club was part of their soul, so once Lehmann was on board we didn't enter the market again until January when Jose Antonio Reyes came in from Sevilla for £10.5m to bolster the forwards. Lehmann was completely different from Seaman in so many ways. Absolutely no disrespect to David, who was probably the best keeper in the league at one time, but he was coming to the end of a distinguished career and was a totally different person. Jens was a very verbal character on the pitch, where David was quiet, controlled and did what he had to with great efficiency. Jens in contrast was talking all the time through matches, warning his back four of potential danger and organising the players in front of him. We liked that. And we liked it even more that we had replaced one outstanding goalkeeper with another.

But the real reason we were such a good team that year was because we had class players all over the pitch; players who were prepared to work hard for each other and who would never give up. It sounds a simple formula but it is rare when all the ingredients come together in one team, as it did in 2003/04 so spectacularly. You can have highly talented, world-class players at your disposal but, if the team ethic is not there, if people don't gel into a team, it won't work.

Arsene realised this from the moment he arrived because he had, in the likes of Steve Bould, Lee Dixon, Martin Keown and Nigel Winterburn, players who knew what it meant to play for Arsenal. They were the tough foundations on which he was able to add wonderful players like Thierry Henry and Robert Pires. Bruce Rioch had brought in Dennis Bergkamp and there's no doubt the foreign players gave us an extra dimension: flair added to a granite core. You don't realise until years later, when you've had the chance to reflect, just how good it was. We went everywhere with the same sense of indestructibility, the refusal to believe we were going to lose. To us that year, going to Anfield and Old Trafford was just another game and we would go there with great confidence and self-belief. No matter who we played, we battled for every ball.

Arsene was just the man to lead this team. Not only was he a great coach but he also had the respect of us all. I enjoyed working with him over many years and never once in all that time did I see him lose his temper. At half-time, if we were not doing especially well – or even if we were – he would 'manage' the game. It sounds simple, but he must have been tempted, as others were, to throw a tea cup or two, but he didn't ever raise his voice. Everything was done with calmness and consideration. If we had problems, he would sort them out on the training pitch on the Monday when tempers had cooled and reason had been restored. Never once did he degrade a player in front of the others, never once did he single anyone out for criticism, and that way he earned and kept their respect. Privately, when the proverbial dust had settled, he might have a quiet word with a player he felt had gone wrong or not performed to known capability and privately he might discuss with me issues regarding a player. But publicly much of his success came as the result of his discretion. He and I had our differences of opinion, though never deep or lingering differences. We were both passionate about Arsenal and wanted us to succeed, but it was never personal and he encouraged me to say what I felt. What the players also knew about Arsene was that he had no favourites. There were no players guaranteed a place no matter how important they seemed to the outsider, not even Thierry. The thing about footballers is that it's not possible for them to be at their best all of the time, so he would not hesitate to take players out and put others in if he felt that was best for the team. That way he ensured the squad was always strong and motivated: play below par and you were out.

Consistency was the key to our eventual success and we had one or two extremely difficult moments. We had Sol Campbell sent off after 25 minutes against Everton on the opening day and David Seaman made a mistake in the Manchester City game to gift Freddie Ljungberg our winner, but the first real controversy came when we were at home to Portsmouth, the sort of team we would have been expected to beat. Teddy Sheringham scored first for Pompey, and there was uproar among their supporters and on their bench when a penalty was given for a foul by Dejan Stefanovic on Robert Pires. Thierry scored to rescue a point but Portsmouth manager Harry Redknapp left Highbury feeling aggrieved, claiming Pires had dived. I have no idea if it was a penalty or not but what I can say is that Robert's control was as good as I have seen in any player. He was a magnificent forward and his great asset was in being able to keep the ball in the tightest of situations, such as this. It would have been dangerous for any defender to have dived in. He would have had to be 100 per cent in his challenge because Robert never lost the ball as far as I can recall. We used to say at Arsenal, 'the safest place on the pitch is in the opposition's penalty area' and in the Premier League you have to be very sure about your tackling.

The match which stands out for many was the goalless draw with Manchester United at Old Trafford. Again, it was hard to be sure from a position in the dug-out exactly what happened but after Patrick Vieira had been sent off for kicking out at Ruud van Nistelrooy, it all got a bit heated. Matches with United are always very fiery and in the last minute they got a penalty. I'm not sure to this day that it was a foul, and Van Nistelrooy hit the bar with his spot kick. All hell broke loose after that and six of our players were charged with improper conduct because of jostling after the final whistle. Lauren got a four-game ban and Keown and Vieira were also suspended. What fans may not realise is what is being said out on the pitch at any given game. Here you had 22 of the best players in the country trying to obtain some sort of advantage and saying things in the heat of battle they probably never meant and would never say in the cold light of day. This was a big, big match and there was nothing we could do to stop the mass fight. United were always incredibly tough opponents and, until the penalty was missed, it looked as if we were going to be deprived by a very dubious refereeing decision. What stood out for me in those clashes with United over the years was the fierce rivalry between Vieira and Roy Keane. It was wonderful to watch because neither gave an inch and yet at the end there were handshakes and smiles and mutual recognition of a wonderful opponent.

We ended 2003 in second place with 45 points from 19 matches and doggedly plodded on until what for me was the biggest match of the season, when we had to avoid defeat against our dear friends at Tottenham to win the title. Our nearest rivals, Chelsea, were at Newcastle on the same day and we daren't slip up. I remember having to keep the Chelsea score away from our players so that the famous Arsenal concentration and diligence was maintained. And it was. Vieira and Pires put us 2-0 up and, although Spurs came back to draw, Chelsea lost at Newcastle after taking the lead and the title was ours. Weird how these things work out, but we had also clinched the 1970/71 championship at White Hart Lane when I was a player in pursuit of our first Double.

So, in the end it all came down to Leicester's visit on the last day. Not in itself an attractive fixture. We were already the champions and, in circumstances like that, Arsene might have been tempted to leave out the big names and try some of the youngsters thirsting for their chance. But here we were, one unbeaten match away from going through the whole season without losing, a feat almost unprecedented. All we had to do was produce the usual Arsenal efficiency, keep working and do our very best. Leicester had nothing to play for.

Anyway, after 26 minutes, Paul Dickov, of all people, put Leicester in front and I think our fans must have wondered if we were about to falter at the last. I knew Dickov only too well. He was one of my FA Youth Cup winners and now here he was about to come back and haunt us on the brink of creating history.

Dickov was a fine young player coming through the system. He was chirpy, always laughing and very much a winner. I had warned our defenders not to get too close to him because he was good at turning in tight situations and he loved the contact element of the game. He had come through the academy system when I was in charge of it with guys like Michael Thomas, Paul Merson, David Rocastle, Steve Morrow and David Hillier. Arsene loved to bring players through from the youth system but never rushed their progress, bringing them in for a game or two and taking them out again so that their assimilation was gradual. We had some fabulous young talent and now one of them was about to ruin it all. Nerves were calmed soon after the break when Henry got a penalty and then, midway through the second-half, Vieira got the winner. I don't think there were any great celebrations at the end, just a recognition that another solid, typical Arsenal performance had been rewarded with a win. Only later did we think what a fantastic achievement it was to go through an entire nine-month campaign without losing. If it ever happens again, it won't happen very often.

We had some great players of course. The unusual back four comprising Lauren, Ashley Cole, Campbell and Kolo Toure was simply outstanding and the midfield of Vieira, Gilberto Silva, Edu and Ljungberg had flair and competitiveness. Up front, Henry, Pires and Bergkamp were three of the finest players of their generation. Henry got 30 goals in 37 appearances in the league that season. He was a lovely guy, modest for a superstar and brilliant to work with. Opponents tried to intimidate him by threatening him and trying all sorts of underhand tricks, but it was actually the worst thing they could have done. He revelled in that sort of banter, upped his game and destroyed one team after another. If I had to offer any advice to any opponent, not that I would have given it, I would have said that whatever you do, don't upset him. In fairness, he would have been the first to acknowledge that he would not have been half as successful without Pires and Bergkamp, who could spot his runs with precision, the sort of precision only top-class players can provide. I'm occasionally asked about the great players of my playing time and if they could have coped with the football of today. I have to say George Best was the best player I ever saw bar none. My most difficult opponent would also have been a sensation today on good pitches and with dangerous tackles eliminated. Eddie Gray of Leeds was a hard man to read because he could go both ways and torment the likes of me, trying to mark him. Eddie suffered from injuries and was a bit in Best's shadow. It didn't help him either to be playing for a club outside the big cities. As assistant manager it was a pleasure to work with the likes of Bergkamp, Henry and Pires and so many others day in and day out and a pleasure too to have had so many happy years at Arsenal. I was simply in the right place at the right time and only now, after it has all gone, do I realise how fortunate I was to have been part of some of the club's golden years.

DAVID SEAMAN

David Seaman
Goalkeeper
1990–2003

Yorkshire born and bred, David Seaman began his career at Leeds, the club he supported devoutly as a youngster. However, his dreams of becoming a star at Elland Road were dashed when he was let go by boyhood hero Eddie Gray in the summer of 1982. Seaman was offered a lifeline by Peterborough United and played 91 league games for the Posh before spells at Birmingham and Queens Park Rangers. It was during his time at QPR that Seaman's talents were spotted by former Arsenal great Bob Wilson, who recommended the future England number one to his old club. Seaman's arrival to replace 1989 hero John Lukic was not universally popular with Arsenal fans but he quickly won them over with a string of stellar displays to help recapture the First Division title in 1991. Upon his arrival at Highbury, George Graham famously declared: 'John Lukic is one of the best goalkeepers in the country but David Seaman is THE Best.' Nicknamed 'Safe Hands' and instantly recognisable owing to his trademark moustache and flowing locks, Seaman's Arsenal trophy cabinet includes three league championships, four FA Cups, a League Cup and a European Cup Winners' Cup. He also helped England to the semi-finals of Euro 96 and is the Three Lions' second most capped goalkeeper after Peter Shilton with 75 appearances. He retired at the age of 40 in January 2004, six months after leaving his beloved Gunners for Kevin Keegan's Manchester City.

Arsenal 1-0 Sheffield United

FA Cup semi-final
Sunday, 12 April 2003
Old Trafford, Manchester
Attendance: 59,170

Arsenal	Sheffield United
Seaman	Kenny
Lauren	Jagielka
Keown	Page
Campbell	Curtis
Cole	Kozluk
Ljungberg	Ndlovu
Edu	Brown
Vieira (Silva)	McCall (Asaba)
Parlour	Tonge
Jeffers (Henry)	Allison (Montgomery)
Wiltord (Bergkamp)	Kabba (Peschisolido)

Managers
Arsene Wenger   Neil Warnock

Goal
Ljungberg

'Arsene who?' That was very much the reaction of all the lads when we discovered the identity of our new manager in September 1996. Nobody had ever heard of Arsene Wenger, so for him to come in and take over a massive club like ours was a huge gamble by the board.

But had it not been for Arsene, and his revolutionary approach to management, I doubt I would have still been around at the age of 39 to make the special save that defines the match of my Arsenal life.

I was lucky because Arsene came in and introduced a whole new way of being a footballer with our diet, our nutrition, our physio, our masseurs and our training. He got us doing a lot of core work, resistance work and rubber band work that certainly added years on to my career, and it was the same for all of our famous back four of Lee Dixon, Martin Keown, Tony Adams and Nigel Winterburn. Without Arsene and his modern methods, we might have been playing lower down the leagues but definitely not in the Premier League for one of the top teams in the country.

What Arsene also did that was very cute of him was bring in players like Nicolas Anelka, Emmanuel Petit, Patrick Vieira, Gilles Grimandi and Remi Garde from France and they were already on his diet, which was alien to the rest of us. It meant we could see players eating a lot of food three hours before a game and thinking they would never be able to run around with that much inside them, but because it was the right food, they were able to go non-stop for 90 minutes. As soon as we witnessed that at first hand all of the other players got straight on to the same diet and it brought instant rewards.

My pre-match meal, before Arsene came in, along with about six other players, consisted of a ham and cheese omelette with baked beans. Ian Wright used to have a fillet steak with a fried egg on top, while others would have beans on toast and scrambled egg. It went from that to pasta with a really light tomato sauce and a choice of steamed fish or steamed chicken and boiled veg and boiled potatoes. On the night before a game we were allowed apple pie with zero-fat yoghurt as a special treat.

Arsene's arrival also brought a return to European football, which called time on our famous Tuesday drinking club. The only reason the Tuesday club appeared was because we used to have Wednesdays off, so we would train hard on a Tuesday morning and then go out and have a couple of beers, but once we started having midweek games that quickly fizzled out.

There was still a good core of English players at the club so we would still have a drink after games and some of the foreign lads used to join in. We were mainly beer and lager drinkers and I remember once Patrick ordered a glass of whisky, which raised a few eyebrows. I asked our lanky French midfielder, 'What are you doing drinking that?' and he said, 'Me drinking one of these is like drinking ten of your pints, Patrick always was one step ahead!

I guess there was a danger by bringing in so many players from one country that cliques could develop in the dressing room and some of the lads did get annoyed if the new signings started speaking French, but that did not last long.

Any player who came in had to earn their right to be in the dressing room and be in our team and we could see straight away on the training ground how talented they all were. Take Nicolas Anelka, for example, who was better than Thierry Henry when they each first arrived. Nicolas was head and shoulders above Henry, but Thierry developed into a much better player.

Nicolas was young and clearly influenced by people outside the game, like agents, and when you look at his career he went to a lot of clubs and did not stay anywhere very long. He was a bit nomadic. I played with him for Arsenal legends against Real Madrid legends once and asked where he was living; he said he was living in the Palm Hotel, one of the most luxurious in Dubai, so things did not work out too badly for him!

As the likes of Thierry arrived, the standard in training became really high and that was mainly down to the fact Arsene had a policy of picking players who were on form in training, not just regulars in the team. If he spotted a player who had done well during the week, he would play them on a Saturday.

We had Thierry, Dennis Bergkamp and Wrighty before them – all fantastic finishers – and that raised my standards as well, knowing that if I could face them in training, there are not many players out there who were better on a match day.

Maybe that helped me when it came to the save I produced to deny Paul Peschisolido a certain goal in this FA Cup semi-final. I knew instinctively it was a good save but did not realise just how good until I watched it back after the match and when everybody starting ringing to congratulate me on it. Even Peter Schmeichel said on TV it was the best save he had ever seen, which coming from him meant so much because we had been such great rivals.

It was a special save, even more so because I was approaching my 40th birthday and had been getting quite a bit of stick from pundits saying I was too old. It was nice to make that save and shut a lot of people up.

The save has had about four million views on YouTube and three million of them are mine. I have watched it back so many times so I can recount it off the top of my head.

The ball had been crossed in and ping-ponged around our box and, when the header from point-blank range finally came, I was conscious of the fact the ball was behind me so knew I could not attempt to catch it as my body momentum would have taken me into the goal along with the ball.

I could not push it out either, because Peschisolido would have just tapped in the rebound, so I decided to claw it away and get it out of the danger zone. These are the moments you put in all the hours of practice for in training, so you can make the correct split-second decisions, although I have to admit I did not realise at the time exactly how close to the line I was.

I remember Ashley Cole coming in and giving me a pat on the cheek to say well done but I did not really react. That was just the way I was. I was not one to celebrate big saves, unless they were in a penalty shoot-out like for England against Spain at Euro 96.

We went on to win the game 1-0 in somewhat controversial circumstances. Freddie Ljungberg scored from a rebound ten minutes before half-time after Sylvain Wiltord had hit the post. I was not aware at the time about all the commotion in the build-up to that goal when first Sheffield United had a player down injured and then referee Graham Poll, who had waved play on, blocked Michael Tonge from getting the ball as we broke upfield. I was a long way from the play and did not have a clue all of that had gone on. I guess I was just caught up in the moment.

The other reason this match stands out in my memories is that it was my 1,000th appearance as a professional, although that did lead to an embarrassing moment for me. After the game I had swapped shirts with Paddy Kenny, the Sheffield United goalkeeper, and it was only when my friends pointed out I might like to keep mine as a memento of my milestone and having made such a great save that I realised I had made a mistake.

On the Monday morning I phoned up Paddy and asked if I could have the shirt back and swap it for another one. I had signed it but luckily enough he did not ask me to write his name so I just wrote 'Safe Hands. David Seaman' on the front of it. Paddy sent it back to me and in return I sent him a couple of my other match-worn shirts and two pairs of my gloves so it turned out okay in the end.

Reaching 1,000 games is not something I could have predicted after being let go by my hometown club Leeds as a 19-year-old. That was a crushing moment for me, being told by one of my idols, Eddie Gray, I was not wanted, and I was thinking, 'What am I going to do now?' because I had put everything into being a footballer.

Luckily, I got a call from Peterborough United to put me back on the right road, because without them I would probably have ended up becoming a baker's delivery boy as my dad owned a grocery and sandwich shop and I used to work for him on a Saturday.

Peterborough was a great club at which to reignite my career because they put me straight into the first team, which was great because, although it was only Fourth Division football, I was playing against men. I was 19 and wafer-thin and had to learn quickly.

From there I went to Birmingham and later Queens Park Rangers, which was where I first started working with Bob Wilson. Bob coached me all the way through from QPR to Arsenal and we became great friends. He is a proper guy and was best man at both of my weddings. It was also Bob who recommended me to George Graham ahead of my move at the start of 1990.

Alex Ferguson was trying to sign me at the same time so I had a choice of Manchester United or Arsenal, but Alex said he could not do it before the summer because he did not want to upset his current goalkeepers so we did a deal with Arsenal, not that it was smooth going.

I was at Highbury waiting to sign my contract and all the press were there too, but John Lukic would not go and he had to leave in order for me to sign, so I ended up going back to QPR and getting a bit of stick from the fans for saying I wanted to leave. Arsenal fans were saying they did not want me because Lukic was better. It was non-stop.

I eventually signed about a week later for a British record fee for a goalkeeper, but I did not feel any pressure from that. The pressure I felt was having to replace Lukic and trying to prove a lot of people wrong – again. I won the league in my first full season of 1990/91, conceding only 18 goals, and of course lifted the FA Cup in my last season, so it was nice to start and finish on a trophy-winning high.

After overcoming Sheffield United we beat Southampton 1-0 in the final in Cardiff with Robert Pires scoring the only goal seven minutes before half-time. I did not have much to do in the game but did make one decent save with my right arm to keep out Brett Ormerod's header towards the end.

The FA Cup has had its critics down the years but even as a kid I used to love cup final day and the wall-to-wall TV coverage that went with it back in the day. As a player it is very different because you are so focused on not making a mistake. You are not even worried about winning, just about trying to play well.

I was captain for the day as Patrick had picked up an injury and that was a great experience, to go to the Millennium Stadium, lead the team out and introduce the players to the VIP guests before the game instead of being introduced. I was only ever captain for England once and that was a great honour, so to do it in an FA Cup Final was absolutely brilliant.

I was fortunate enough to win two finals at the old Wembley and that was such a special place when you think about what had happened there: England winning the World Cup, Live Aid and all sorts of other big concerts. Cardiff as a venue was very different but still good and the atmosphere was always electric, especially if the retractable roof was on, making it very echoey inside.

At the end of the match, Patrick came on to the pitch in his cup final suit and we had a bit of a row because I wanted him to come up and collect the cup with me. He said: 'No. It is your day.' I said: 'If you don't go up, I won't go up.' I won the argument and we went up and lifted it together.

Patrick was club captain and I was vice-captain. We had a really good friendship and I felt it was right for him to be there as he had been a massive part of us getting to the final. Patrick was a gentle giant, a really nice guy, but once he was on that pitch, he had a tough streak about him. He would put his foot in and anything else for that matter, including his elbows.

As well as being a big personality, Patrick was a very tall guy in keeping with a lot of our team at that time. Arsene wanted his players to be athletes even before being good footballers and, whenever we travelled to an away ground, we would always see the apprentices waiting for us at the entrance to the tunnel and they would remark to each other about how big we all were.

I did not know at that time that the final was also to be my last game for Arsenal and it was not until the summer that I realised things were not going to work out as I had hoped.

I was on the beach in Portugal when I got a call from Arsene. He said: 'David, I have an offer for you; I want you to be my number three goalkeeper.' I was shocked, but ready to reluctantly agree. He also said he wanted me to be his goalkeeping coach, which would have sweetened the deal as going into coaching, especially at Arsenal, interested me, but then he told me there would be a 75 per cent wage drop!

I just started laughing and he knew I had clubs chasing me. My contract was up and I had offers from Manchester City and a couple of others so I chose Man City because I still felt and believed I could do it for at least another year and in some ways I wanted to prove Arsene wrong, just like I had wanted to prove Eddie Gray wrong much earlier in my career.

By the time Arsene's phone call came, I had already gone through about three one-year contracts with Arsenal. I used to sign at the end of each season just for one year and that worked for me.

I was disappointed, there was no doubt about that, because I wanted to stay at Arsenal but always knew that at some stage it would come to an end. I was getting a few more injuries and at my age it was taking a little bit longer to come back. I knew somebody would be coming in, although at that stage I did not know Jens Lehmann had been lined up, so I was not angry at all and Arsene and I have met lots of times since and it has always been very amicable, reminiscing about the great memories we shared.

That is the cuteness of Arsene Wenger; he knows when players are past it and when they need moving on. He did it with a lot of players like Wrighty and even Thierry when he went to Barcelona, and other big players like Petit and Marc Overmars.

I was a little bit sad I did not get to say goodbye but, even though I only lasted six months at City before deciding to call it a day, at least I got to play against Arsenal for them. It was early in the season and we lost 2-1 at home. My biggest worry was remembering not to catch the ball and instinctively throw it straight to an Arsenal player.

I was injured for the reverse fixture at Highbury but I still got a guard of honour from both sets of players before the match. I walked out with my daughter in my arms and that was a nice thing to do, because I never really got to say thank you to the Arsenal fans.

I break my Arsenal career down into two sections: the time before Arsene and the time after. Even before his arrival we had won the league, the domestic cup Double and the Cup Winners' Cup, which a lot of people forget because they think football did not exist before the Premier League.

The big difference between Arsene and George Graham is that Arsene had better players at his disposal, a lot of whom he recruited himself. George's squad was not massively talented but gelled together as a team. We did not play the most attractive football and a lot of it was long ball and possession-based, but he got the best out of us and that is why he won what he did.

Arsene was totally different. As soon as he arrived, he demanded that we played it out from the back and that made me very nervous because I just wanted my defenders to hoof it away, but it worked and he got us playing Total Football.

He also had a fantastic eye for a player and the summer before the 2002/03 season Gilberto Silva and Kolo Toure arrived and would both go on to become Invincibles. Gilberto was a quiet man but should have got a lot more credit, because he was a brilliant defensive midfielder. You do not become a Brazilian international by accident. Kolo was a very raw talent when he first came. We used to play eight versus eight in training and he would be running around everywhere; he was like the little boy in the playground who would just follow the ball. We would all be screaming at him to stay in position and eventually he learned and became a great player.

We finished runners-up in the league that year and at that time when we always seemed to be close. If we did not win it, Man United won it and if they didn't win it, we did. It was a good time to be an Arsenal fan, because we were always there or thereabouts.

Arsene did not just change it for Arsenal but for English football in general and even United benefited from his impact. When we went away on England duty the United players would be sat on one table for lunch and us Arsenal players on another. Our club doctor, John Crane, was also the England doctor and we would all still be following the Arsene diet. I remember Gary Neville looking over one day and saying: 'Doc, what are they eating? We should all be eating the same.' They took it back to United and the next thing we knew, they were all on the same diet.

Suddenly nobody was asking, 'Arsene who?' any more.

ALAN SMITH

Alan Smith
Forward
1987–1995

Alan 'Smudger' Smith is a name synonymous with two of the greatest nights in Arsenal's modern history. His goal at Anfield, detailed elsewhere in this book, set the Gunners on the way to their remarkable last-day 1989 title triumph. Five years later Smith was the match-winner as George Graham's men ended a 24-year wait for a European trophy by beating a star-studded Parma side in the Cup Winners' Cup Final. Smith was first spotted by Leicester City playing for non-league Alvechurch and went on to form a formidable partnership with England legend Gary Lineker to lead the Foxes to promotion to Division One. He moved to Highbury in March 1987 before being loaned back to Leicester for the remainder of the season and went on to score 86 league goals in Arsenal red, twice ending the season as the top-flight's leading marksman. After retiring in 1995, Smith, who was capped 13 times by England, forged a new career as a much-respected television pundit with Sky Sports and a writer for the *Daily Telegraph*.

Arsenal 1-0 Parma

European Cup Winners' Cup Final
Wednesday, 4 May 1994
Parken Stadium, Copenhagen
Attendance: 33,765

Arsenal	**Parma**
Seaman	Bucci
Dixon	Benarrivo
Adams	Apolloni
Bould	Sensini
Winterburn	Di Chiara
Davis	Minotti
Selley	Pin (Melli)
Morrow	Brolin
Campbell	Crippa
Smith	Zola
Merson (McGoldrick)	Asprilla

Managers

George Graham — Nevio Scala

Goal

Smith

Whenever I am asked to recount the best moment of my career, Anfield in 89 always comes out on top. No matter how long you play for you are never going to beat winning the league in such dramatic circumstances, but Copenhagen was the next best thing.

In many ways I regard that night in the Danish capital as a port in the storm, because it came at a time in my career that I do not look back on with too much fondness. I was struggling for confidence and not scoring goals as frequently as I would have liked. Ian Wright had recently come to the club and we did not really click as a duo because he was such a one-off and therefore was difficult to anticipate and read, which affected my confidence and meant life became more miserable on and off the pitch.

To be able to put all that aside and roll back the years was a lovely feeling and to crown it with a goal in the final of a major European competition, only my second of the calendar year, made it even more special.

Just reaching the final was a big achievement in itself as we had to account for some very good sides along the way, including Torino in the quarter-finals. The first leg of that tie, played in the soulless, cavernous bowl we know as the Stadio delle Alpi, was a draining night because there were not many fans inside and that place feels empty even when there are 30,000 there.

It was a dreadful game of very few chances; I remember I got man-marked and it was just a running battle with my centre-half. It finished 0-0 and then back at Highbury we won 1-0, with our captain fantastic Tony Adams getting the all-important goal with a header from a set piece.

Next up it was on to Paris where we came away from the first leg with a 1-1 draw against Paris St Germain, a more than acceptable result, particularly given our hosts had gone 35 matches unbeaten coming into the game. We scored first through another set-piece header, this time from Wrighty, before David Ginola, later to grace the Premier League with our bitter rivals

Tottenham and Newcastle, equalised with a glancing header from a near-post corner.

I will never forget that goal because Steve Bould and big Tony had been giving Ginola stick all match. After he scored, he wheeled away to celebrate before remembering and doubled back on himself to give them some back in return!

It was during that game in the French capital the famous 'One-nil to the Arsenal' chant got its first airing because they played 'Go West' by the Pet Shop Boys on the public address system at half-time and our fans starting singing 'One-nil'.

That is where it all started and we did get 1-0 in the return leg thanks to Kevin Campbell's early goal. Not for the first time that year we rode our luck and they had some good chances, including one from Ginola. They were a strong side with some very good players but were without the great George Weah for the second match, which probably did us a favour.

The final itself was scheduled for the Parken Stadium, home of FC Copenhagen, where I was to return several years later working for *The Telegraph* to cover Arsenal's UEFA Cup Final defeat to Galatasaray. That was a very different experience to my first visit and I remember there was a problem with the internet so I had to scramble around underneath the desk and around people's feet with all dust on the floor, trying desperately to get a connection to file my full-time match report. It is quite funny when you think about it.

There was a lot of excitement when we arrived in Denmark because, being a final, we expected to find ourselves staying in a swanky hotel, but we were all a bit disappointed with what greeted us. The club had booked us into a place just outside Copenhagen because they wanted somewhere quiet where fans were not going to wake us up in the middle of the night. It was quite basic to say the least and we were hoping for a better standard of accommodation.

I was sharing with Alan Miller, our back-up goalkeeper, who became my room-mate after Anders Limpar left the club, and we just had a bog-standard room containing two beds, a wardrobe and a bedside table. It was the kind of place we would usually stop in during a pre-season training camp. Still, at least we got a decent night's sleep before the big match.

We were massive underdogs because Parma were a wonderful team, blessed with talents like Gianfranco Zola, Faustino Asprilla and Tomas Brolin as well as several members of the Italian squad that would reach the final of the World Cup in America a couple of months later.

They were holders of the trophy, bidding to become the first side to win it in consecutive seasons, and our cause was not helped by the fact we were missing Wrighty, our top scorer. That was a huge blow because he was the one getting the majority of our goals that season. Wrighty had been booked in the first half of the second leg of our semi-final against PSG and knew he would be banned from playing in the final if we got there under the totting-up process.

He was inconsolable in the dressing room at half-time and the lads and George Graham had to work really hard to calm him down because we needed him for the second half. He was gutted about potentially missing such a showpiece occasion but we still had a job to do and, to be fair to Wrighty, he knuckled down and helped us to get over the line.

It was hard for him in the days building up to the final and we all knew how he was feeling inside, especially someone like Wrighty, who was such an emotional character at the best of times. He tried to put a brave face on it and be just as bubbly as usual around the team. We, as team-mates, all felt sorry for him.

In his absence it was like going back to the years before we signed Wrighty, who, like me, had made his name in non-league football with Greenwich Borough before being given his route into the professional game by Crystal Palace. I was deployed as the central striker, with Paul Merson on one side and Kevin Campbell the other. I did not feel any extra pressure even though the goals had started to dry up for me. I just wanted to give my best performance.

Martin Keown also failed a fitness test on the day of the game too and John Jensen had suffered a cruciate knee injury and was not available either so we were light on numbers, but thankfully we still had our usual back five in place and they were fantastic on the night, just when we needed them the most.

George had made a decision at the start of the season to adopt a 4-3-3 system in Europe, a tactical switch which had come about as a result of being knocked out of the European Cup in the second round by Benfica three years earlier when he felt we were too open. It meant we would play 4-4-2 in the Premier League on a Saturday and then come into London Colney on the Monday and work on our new shape for the upcoming midweek game.

It took a bit of getting used to as we had been so successful playing the more traditional way and I have to admit some of us did question why we were changing. There was also the need for a bit of patience on the training ground as George virtually had to walk us through what he wanted us to do.

In that formation there was always an onus on the wide boys to funnel back when we did not have the ball and make it a five-man midfield to ensure we were very tight and resilient, just how George loved his teams to be. I was the focal point of attack, the target to try and hold the ball up to give my team-mates time to get up the pitch.

It was hard work because you would be standing next to one centre-half, make a run and end up standing next to the other, but it played to my strengths in terms of having my back to goal and it was never a struggle for me to play that way.

Players had a moan at first and it was a bit different as there were not many teams in the Premier League playing that way back then, but, like anything, if something is successful you buy into it and it was successful, taking us all the way to the final that season and again the following year when we narrowly failed to retain the trophy, losing to Spanish side Real Zaragoza and Nayim's infamous goal from the halfway line.

It was almost like a home game when we went out to warm up before kick-off as three quarters of the ground was taken up by Arsenal fans. There was only a pocket of Parma supporters and our banners and flags were everywhere. There was red and white as far as the eye could see and after we had won and were celebrating that made it really special.

My match-winning moment came in the 20th minute and is one I still recall vividly. Lee Dixon gave the ball to me from a throw-in and I laid it back, he then hoisted it forward looking for Mers and I thought the move was going to come to an end only for one of their defenders to attempt a strange, overhead kick clearance which landed straight at my chest. It was a bit of an awkward one because I controlled it towards the top of my chest and the ball bounced up high, so I knew I would have to take the shot earlier than I normally would because the defenders were closing me down quickly.

I skipped on to it and volleyed it quite high on my left foot. I knew I had connected well with the ball but it was only when their goalkeeper had dived and landed that I realised it was in. I assumed it must have hit the inside of the post, because I glimpsed it rolling across the line and into the back of the net.

That was a brilliant moment and a time to celebrate but I was conscious there was still a lot of the match left to play. From that point on we were a bit fortunate, because Parma had a goal chalked off for offside and Lee Dixon could easily have given away a penalty; he still laughs about that now because he virtually chopped somebody in two inside the 18-yard box and amazingly the referee waved play on.

We needed our goalkeeper on top form and Dave Seaman, who was playing through a bit of pain after having injections in his injured ribs, made some good saves too. One of Dave's biggest strengths was that he never got ruffled, he was always very calm, with that trademark big grin. As a person he was like you would see in public and had a jovial personality but was always steady in his temperament.

John Lukic was a very good keeper and we were all surprised and disappointed when we discovered the gaffer was going to replace him having won the league with John in 1989, but Dave was a notch above, he was top class and saved us in so many games.

After I scored I spent much of the evening watching Parma going forward and hoping our defenders could hold out for the clean sheet. I was always confident they would because we had seen them do it so many times before.

That back four was comfortably the best I ever played with in my career and the most amazing thing is that they stayed together for so long. I was there at the start when George would have me trying to break them down in training along with Mers, David Rocastle and Brian Marwood, and if we got through once it would be a major achievement and we would be running around the training pitch celebrating.

We worked with organisation of the back four in mind so much that if George said, 'We are going to concentrate on defending today lads', they would think, 'Oh no. Not again!' but they appreciated it because they just had a telepathic understanding of where each other would be. It was such a brilliant unit the like of which we will probably never see again, because players do not hang around at one club for long enough these days.

The celebrations after the game were fairly low-key as we flew home that night, which we were all gutted about as we would have loved to have stayed in Copenhagen. We had our final Premier League game at Newcastle the following weekend and, had we lost the final, we would have needed to get something there to qualify for Europe the next season so the directors did not want to take any chances.

We had a few glasses of champagne on the flight, had a sleep and got back to a deserted Stansted Airport at about four o'clock in the morning. It did feel a bit of an anticlimax and not how we would have wanted it.

We went to Newcastle on the Friday and there was a wedding taking place at our hotel, so a few of the lads decided they would pop down and join in. Andy Linighan was one of them and George feared the worst because he could remember what he was like as a player when he would have been straight down there congratulating the bride with a drink or two!

In the end George sent his assistant, Stewart Houston, to check all our rooms and make sure we were behaving ourselves. 'Maxy' Miller and me had just ordered two Budweisers each and Stewart saw them and read the riot act. I said to him: 'Stewart, do us a favour. This game tomorrow means nothing and we have just won the Cup Winners' Cup!' In the end he relented and told us to make sure we stopped at two bottles. The next day we lost 2-0, not that anybody really cared too much.

My relationship with George was good for most of my Arsenal career but tailed off a bit towards the end when I had stopped scoring and he was getting frustrated as the cycle with that team had clearly come to an end.

He was always a tough taskmaster but I was a good trainer, never gave him any trouble and we got on well; there was a real respect there.

Maybe when Arsene Wenger came in as manager and was tearing it up with the Invincibles George's achievements were overlooked, but subsequently people now look back on that time with a lot of fondness and recognise what golden years they were and what a special time it was.

George had so much work to do when he arrived at the club and had to get rid of a lot of players so he was fortunate to inherit a good youth team and was able to bring through the likes of Tony Adams, David Rocastle, Mickey Thomas and Mers. He made a lot of changes and was really successful.

Our team had a lot of spirit and a lot of fight and we were not a side who would be rolled over and bullied; obviously there have been times recently where that has not always been the case with Arsenal and I think fans appreciate that.

As well as being a good tactician, George was clever in that he would give the players a little bit of leeway and recognised it was good for our team spirit to let us go out and enjoy ourselves.

On a Tuesday, if we did not have a midweek game, we would do a physical session at Highbury where we would run around the track, have sprint races up to the top of the North Bank, go to the gym and do some weights and play a five-a-side match. On one of those Tuesdays somebody suggested we go for a drink and that was how the famous Tuesday club was born. The gaffer always knew what was going on, because he could see we had brought smarter clothes with us than we normally would and they were hanging up in the dressing room, although none of us could get near David Rocastle's wardrobe. Rocky set the standard and was immaculate, unlike Tony Adams, who wore some dodgy gear. Tony had this black leather duffle coat with a hood, which drew a few funny comments.

We would come back from the gym, jump in the shower and would all be buzzing because we knew we were going out for a little drink afterwards. It was great for togetherness and most of the lads did get involved. George always told us to enjoy ourselves but to do it responsibly, as he did not want to receive any letters about us misbehaving.

They were great days and I am proud to look back at all the medals I won. You can be the best footballer in the world but if you join a club at the wrong time then maybe your trophy cabinet can end up empty; however, I joined Arsenal at the beginning of things so I guess it is all about timing.

FRANK McLINTOCK

Frank McLintock
Defender
1964–1973

Frank McLintock was learning, at his mother's insistence, how to become a fully qualified painter and decorator by the time he left his home city of Glasgow to join Leicester in 1956 as a teenager. McLintock, a calm, authoritative defender and born leader, joined Arsenal when Billy Wright was manager in October 1964 for £80,000. In nine productive years at Highbury, McLintock was captain of Bertie Mee's side which ended a 17-year trophy drought by winning the Inter-Cities Fairs Cup in 1970 and then the coveted League and FA Cup Double a year later. This ended a miserable sequence of cup-final failures for McLintock, who was twice a beaten FA Cup finalist at Leicester and had twice lost in League Cup finals with Arsenal before his luck changed for the better. McLintock was Footballer of the Year in 1971 and was also made an MBE the same year. Later McLintock was sold to Queens Park Rangers by Mee in 1973 for £25,000 and three years later almost added another league title to his collection. QPR were runners-up to Liverpool. When McLintock retired in 1977 aged 38, he had accumulated 766 appearances in 20 years and had scored 66 goals. Oddly overlooked by his country, he won nine Scottish caps and managed Leicester and Brentford. McLintock goes back to the Double-winning year for the match of his life, the victory at Tottenham which sealed the league title as a prelude to winning the FA Cup at Wembley a few days later. In particular he remembers just how tired he was at the end of a magnificent journey.

Tottenham 0-1 Arsenal

Division One
Monday, 3 May 1971
White Hart Lane, London
Attendance: 51,992

Tottenham	Arsenal
Jennings	Wilson
Beal	Rice
Kinnear	McLintock
Knowles	Simpson
Perryman	McNab
Collins	Armstrong
Mullery	Kelly
Neighbour	Kennedy
Peters	George
Chivers	Radford
Gilzean (Pearce)	Graham

Managers

Bill Nicholson   Bertie Mee

Goal

Kennedy

We were all exhausted by the end of that 1970/71 season. By the time you added 42 league games to cups, domestic and European, and various replays, not to mention pre-season friendlies, we must have played 70-odd games and, of course, the nearer we got to winning the Double, the greater the tension. In those days we only had small squads; in our case we only used 16 players in the league that season and the stats show that George Armstrong, myself and Bob Wilson played every game. John Radford, Pat Rice, Bob McNab and Ray Kennedy missed only one and Peter Storey missed two. No wonder we were so tired. But where limbs became heavy and the burden grew, we were fuelled by adrenaline and the sheer determination to succeed.

I had been in this position before. At Leicester – unfancied Leicester – when in 1961 we were third in the league and had a place in the FA Cup Final, against Spurs of all people, going into the last few weeks. But, for whatever reason, we tripped up and fell at the last hurdle. We couldn't sustain our league form and Len Chalmers broke a leg in the final, which ended in a 2-0 defeat.

What's more, by now, in 1971, I was getting fed up with losing important matches. We had also lost to Manchester United in the FA Cup Final of 1963 when I was at Leicester and, at Arsenal, Leeds had beaten us in the League Cup Final of 1968 and Third Division Swindon had seen us off on a mud-heap Wembley a year later. Until we won the Inter-Cities Fairs Cup, I was accumulating a lot of unwanted runners-up trophies.

Now there was this chance to do what only Tottenham, our great rivals, had done in the 20th century, and that was to win the League and FA Cup Double. I was just hoping we wouldn't do another 'Leicester' and buckle under the late pressure, but when you looked at our squad, small though it was, there was great quality and experience in every position and strong characters.

Going into that momentous last week of the 1970/71 season we knew exactly what we had to do. We had to beat Tottenham on their own ground or draw 0-0. A defeat or a score draw would hand the title to Don Revie's talented but combative Leeds. This was on the Monday and on the Saturday we were due to play Liverpool in the FA Cup Final at Wembley. It was going to be the toughest few days of our careers, but we were ready for it.

Bertie Mee was the manager but he realised his limitations as the club's ex-physiotherapist with no real footballing background and let first Dave Sexton and later Don Howe do the coaching. They were shrewd appointments with Bertie keeping out the way while Sexton and Howe coached but being on hand to dish out any discipline required. Howe was my next-door neighbour and was often injured when I first joined Arsenal and it was a shock when he was elevated to the coaching role. We must have played him up a bit at first but then one day he lost his temper and shouted: 'You can f*ck off if you don't want to be here. Go back to the dressing room and I'll get you transferred.' After that, it soon settled and, like Dave, he was a terrific coach.

There were not many miles between Tottenham's ground and our own and, hard to imagine though it might be, we actually got on very well with the Spurs players. We lived near each other and often met at charity golf days and other social occasions. But, believe me, Spurs were very fired up for this big match. There was not much in it for them but they were incredibly motivated. The last thing they wanted was to hand the league title to Arsenal, least of all on their own pitch, and to share with us the great distinction of winning the Double. There was no way they would roll over and do us any favours.

But first we had to get to White Hart Lane. That night there were almost 52,000 inside the ground and I have seen estimates of 30,000–40,000 locked out, unable to get in to witness this stupendous north London occasion. Our coach must have stopped a dozen times as we made a very slow journey through the throng, people banging on the sides and gesticulating. At one point I saw my wife, Barbara, walking towards the ground, trying to get through this sea of fans. I think there were one or two other wives also, so I told the bus driver to stop to let them on. As they boarded, thankful to be rescued, Bertie tut-tutted. I told him to f*ck off. I guess it was the tension.

When we got there at last, the pitch was a big diamond of mud even in May. It was going to be hard to play decent football on but in those days we accepted the fact that all pitches were like that by the end of the season. Oh, for the smooth green surfaces of today.

Spurs were very much up for this. They tore into us from the start. Even Alan Gilzean, a player not noted for his work rate, ran 15 yards to make a challenge and Alan Mullery was putting himself about in midfield with great gusto. It was a fierce old game, full of passion and commitment. Spurs threw everything at us and chased every ball, but I thought we had that little bit of extra class when it mattered. Pat Jennings, later a great player for us, made some good saves and I think we held the edge, but the longer the match went on and there were no goals, it looked as if we might have to settle for a goalless draw.

But with about 12 minutes to go I was convinced I was about to get the winner. I smashed in an absolute cracker of a shot, which was goalbound until it struck the referee and knocked him over. I think he thought I was going to help him to his feet; instead he got a volley of abuse, the only printable word of which was 'idiot'. It wasn't his fault, of course, but that could well have been a sensational goal and made me a hero.

Ray Kennedy was that hero I should have been, heading in an Armstrong cross with three minutes to go. Then mayhem. The crowd invaded and we got off as soon as we could find a way through the invading mob. One down, one to go.

We had a lot of unsung heroes in that team and it was fitting that two of them combined for the winner. There was no fitter, more industrious, more capable winger than Armstrong. He got up and down that left wing match after match and he was also the nicest, kindest person you'll ever meet. Always the first to buy a round of drinks, he would have bought the second if we had let him. How he never played for England, I will never know, and it was a huge tragedy that he should die so young after suffering a brain haemorrhage while taking a training session as a coach at Arsenal aged only 56.

Another mystery was how Port Vale, locked for so long in the lower divisions, let Kennedy go. They decided he was not good enough, but for us he was a sensation, scoring 19 goals in the league alone that season. He was a strange boy, kept himself to himself, and when he arrived we knew nothing about him other than that Port Vale had bombed him out. He and John Radford played so well together, scoring vital goals and dragging defenders all over the pitch. They were a terrific pair.

They should have been recognised by England far more than they were. Radford played only twice, McNab four times and Armstrong and Peter Simpson not at all. They were great players, all of them. The rumour was that Alf Ramsey didn't like Arsenal but I find that hard to believe.

Anyway, there was no time for proper celebrations. The Spurs players were gutted and that made our success all the sweeter but, while they slinked off into the night, we had a big game coming up and Bill Shankly stoked the fires by congratulating us and at the same time saying Liverpool would be far harder to beat at Wembley in a few days' time.

Bill had this habit of being provocative without being rude. He tried to sign me for Liverpool just after Leicester had missed the Double so agonisingly. He approached me, illegally, and said: 'How would you like to play for a good team?' Ian St John, who

I knew from Scotland under-23s, was with him and Bill then started talking in glowing terms of his giant centre-half Ron Yeats. 'He's a colossus, Frank, come and play alongside him.' That was the last I heard from him.

On the Thursday I had to attend a black-tie dinner in the West End where I was made the Football Writers' Association's Footballer of the Year, a proud personal achievement and one I shall always treasure. But I recall going home around 11pm and not being able to sleep until about 4am because I was tired and tense. It's not easy standing up in front of big crowds and making a speech and that only added to my exhaustion.

So come the Saturday and Liverpool at Wembley I was absolutely whacked. The pitch was lovely, the occasion massive and there I was up against 6ft 3in John Toshack, a formidable target man, and I had to find a way of out-jumping him when my legs were lumps of lead and all I wanted to do was go home for a long rest.

I seem to remember George Graham, nobody's idea of a fitness fanatic, was superb for us that day and so, too, the underestimated Radford. The match will always be remembered for Charlie George's winning goal, of course, but it was a typical efficient Arsenal performance which saw us through 2-1.

I think we had a few drinks that night after I had gone up the steps at Wembley to receive the cup, but there was no chance of relaxation. The domestic season over, I put away my winners' medals and headed off to join the Scotland international party for three close-season internationals.

Every player loves playing for their country, but I had had enough after a very hectic, demanding ten months.

Bertie Mee took it upon himself to start breaking up the Double team a year or two later. Four or five of us moved on. Graham, Radford, Kennedy, Armstrong, George and myself were all allowed to leave when we still had more to give. Jeff Blockley came in to replace me and I had to play in five or six games for the reserves until I got my transfer to QPR in 1973. I remember playing in the first reserve game in front of a handful of fans and just kicking the ball anywhere because I was so upset after all I had done for the club. So, I said to myself: 'You can't do that. Give 100 per cent. Be professional.'

I think Bertie made a big mistake letting so many of us go. But I had had nearly ten years at Arsenal and I had to be very grateful for that. I might have gone elsewhere when I was at Leicester: Shankly was one who didn't follow up his initial interest and Don Revie, boss at Leeds, came down to my house at midnight to make me an offer. I was earning £20 a week. He offered me £60 and an £8,000 signing-on fee, which was a huge amount in those days. Again, it was illegal, and again I never heard anything more.

It was not the only time the controversial Revie tried to make me an offer I couldn't refuse. Leeds were intense rivals of ours in those days. They had some marvellous footballers but had a deserved reputation for dishing it out and some of it not always in the spirit of the game.

When they and ourselves were chasing the Double we played Leeds at home. In a very busy and noisy foyer at Highbury, Revie approached me. He asked me how my wife, Barbara, was and asked after our children. He always remembered names and could be very pleasant company. But then he said: 'Take it easy tonight, Frank.' I couldn't hear properly over the din, but when I asked him to repeat what I thought he had said, he whispered: 'Take it easy, Frank. You and Barbara can go anywhere in the world you want.'

I exploded. I knew what he meant only too well and shouted obscenities after him as he turned and fled to the sanctuary of the Leeds dressing room.

But overall, I had some great times at Arsenal. It was a disappointingly low-key ending but things rarely work out exactly the way you planned them. I can look back on some of the happiest and most successful years of my career and I shall always appreciate what we did.

LEE DIXON

Lee Dixon
Defender
1988–2002

Lee Dixon had a rocky, unorthodox road to Arsenal but once he got there he stayed 14 years and clocked up the best part of 500 appearances as a key member of one of the club's best teams in a trophy-laden era. Manchester-born Dixon was rejected by his first club, Burnley, and had to make his way back to the First Division via Chester, Bury and Stoke. Manager George Graham was an avid reader of the regional Saturday evening sports papers and noted how Dixon was consistently voted man of the match by Stoke fans. Taking a close look for himself, Graham promptly paid £765,000 for Dixon and Steve Bould. As first-choice right-back, Dixon won the league four times, the FA Cup three times and also tasted success in the European Cup Winners' Cup. Capped 22 times by England, Dixon retired aged 38 after Arsenal's Double year of 2001/2002. Few matches evoke as much emotion among Arsenal fans and those who played in it than the sensational last-minute win at Anfield in 1989 where Liverpool were seconds away from completing their own League and FA Cup Double. This incredible occasion is Dixon's match of his life.

Liverpool 0-2 Arsenal

Division One
Friday, 26 May 1989
Anfield, Liverpool
Attendance: 41,783

Liverpool	Arsenal
Grobbelaar	Lukic
Ablett	Dixon
Nicol	O'Leary
Hansen	Bould (Groves)
Staunton	Adams
Houghton	Winterburn
Whelan	Thomas
McMahon	Rocastle
Barnes	Richardson
Aldridge	Merson (Hayes)
Rush (Beardsley)	Smith

Managers

Kenny Dalglish   George Graham

Goals

Smith
Thomas

For sheer drama it would be hard to think of a match more spine-tingling than this one. To win the league, we had to go to Anfield and beat Liverpool by two clear goals. Going into the game, the last of a long 38-match season, we were three points behind and Liverpool, having beaten Everton to win the FA Cup, were on the threshold of a Double. They rarely lost at home and were in blistering form, having just dispatched West Ham 5-1. They were clearly very firm favourites since all they had to do was avoid defeat or, at the very worst, only lose 1-0. Not many teams got more than one goal at Liverpool.

In retrospect, it should never have got to this. We had dominated the league for most of the season and should have won it with points to spare but, as Liverpool's challenge grew in momentum, our own form took an alarming dip at just the wrong time. Before going up to Anfield for that fateful showdown, we were beaten at home by Derby and then held to a draw by a modest Wimbledon side. This allowed Liverpool to overtake us just when we had reason to think the title was in our grasp. Before the Derby game, I walked down Avenell Road towards Highbury and I saw one of those roadside tradesman, the sort who sell badges, programmes and scarves in club colours, touting a little badge that said 'Arsenal, 1989 Champions'. More than a little premature, and I remember thinking after we had lost to Derby how he must be sweating on our next two results.

To put it in perspective, this match with Liverpool was very much a contrast in experience. Every man in that Liverpool squad was battle-hardened and knowledgeable and managed by the great Kenny Dalglish. Our squad was newly assembled by George Graham and I was among several for whom this was our first full season in the top flight. George demanded and got complete loyalty and no dissent. He added to the hunger of the academy lads coming through, like Paul Merson, David Rocastle and Michael Thomas, players like myself who had been brought in from the lower divisions with a point to prove. George got me, Bouldy and Nigel Winterburn for about £1m and Kevin Richardson came in cheaply from Everton. To make room for us, this new team, George had removed some of the older players who might not have responded so readily to his harsh regime and strict discipline. In many respects we had done well even to have been challenging for the league championship.

After losing to Derby, it was by no means doom and gloom. George wasn't happy but he thought, reasonably enough, that we would beat Wimbledon. But after only managing a draw, the scene in our dressing room was abject. Among the slumped shoulders, you could hear muttering about having blown it. The chairman came in and virtually conceded the title to Liverpool. 'We've had a great season, lads, but it looks like we've lost our chance.' But here we must credit the manager. While everyone else connected with Arsenal was ready to agree with the chairman, George refused to give up. He's a stubborn man, stoical and brave, and he told us the race was not yet won and lost. We could still go to Liverpool and win. We all wanted to believe him. Our heads told us the statistics were against us but our hearts told us it could be done.

The fixture had been delayed a couple of weeks because of the Hillsborough catastrophe in which 96 died. Liverpool, as a city, was in mourning for this horrendous loss of life, but Liverpool as a football club had gone on this great run of victories and now they were in this tremendous position whereby they could afford to lose and still be champions. Maybe this affected their attitude. They didn't have to win and that may have worked in our favour.

George decided we should travel on the day of the match, rather than linger in Liverpool for a day or two with their fans telling us we were going to lose, and that proved to be a shrewd piece of psychology, because we were relaxed and joking with each other as we drove north. We were playing cards and laughing as if we were going up for a jolly.

The atmosphere was tremendous, as it always is at Anfield, but if there were any nerves, they were not so much in the Arsenal camp.

George knew that Liverpool liked to get off to a fast start, get a goal or two and then play their football, so he picked a team designed to frustrate Dalglish's attacking inclinations. Ian Rush and John Aldridge were scoring for fun but they owed much of their success to the wide players, John Barnes and Ray Houghton. Myself and Nigel Winterburn were told to push up to augment the midfield and get close to the creators. George was ahead of his time in the flexibility of his tactics. In the league we played 4-4-2 but in Europe he liked to go with a 4-3-3 and he would always vary his line-up to counter opponents.

Barnes was a great player, so intelligent, and to simply stop him playing was no easy task. But I was told to stick close to him and deny him space, not to let him turn and run at our defence. Commentators at this match live on ITV were surprised to see George play three centre-halves when Arsenal had to win, but he knew exactly what he was doing. He was so technically clever and astute. There was no questioning what he did by any of our players. George ruled with the proverbial rod of iron and you did as you were told or you were out of the door.

So, Nigel and myself pushed into midfield alongside Rocastle, Richardson and Thomas and Liverpool couldn't get going or impose themselves on us in the way they would have liked. 'Get us to 0-0 at half-time and we can score two in the second half,' George told us.

Before the start, as a gesture of solidarity, each Arsenal player took a bunch of flowers out on to the pitch and gave them to fans in the crowd. I think it was our Managing Director Ken Friar's idea and was a bit of a masterstroke. I ran instinctively to the

Kop end of that historic ground and handed my bunch of flowers to a woman at the front. In a strange kind of way, I remember thinking how we were intruding on their grief but, as a public relations exercise, it did us no harm whatsoever. As I went to the Kop I was reminded fleetingly how, as a young Manchester City fan, I would be passed down to the front over the heads of Liverpool supporters so that I could get a better view. Manchester City invariably lost at Anfield and there I was stuck in the middle of them all. But they were always very kind even to a diminutive opposition fan.

Once we got into game mode, everything else was forgotten. We quickly settled into our game plan and Liverpool struggled to make their usual impact or to create any worthwhile openings. So far, so good.

Then after 52 minutes, we were awarded an indirect free kick and Alan Smith glanced it home just inside a post. One-nil to the Arsenal. Liverpool's players went berserk. We tried to celebrate but we had to keep one eye on the referee, David Hutchinson, who was overwhelmed by an irate red swarm of abuse. They were beside themselves with fury.

At one stage, I thought the referee was going to disallow the goal. The stronger teams tend to do what Liverpool did at that moment, attempt to intimidate and browbeat a referee, and they managed to get him to consult his assistant. For a few seconds we held our breaths. But much to Liverpool's disappointment, the beleaguered official stuck to his decision and we could get on with the rest of the game, which had more than half an hour left to run.

Mr Hutchinson later admitted that he didn't actually know what Liverpool were complaining about. At first we thought they were claiming Smith had not touched the ball, which TV replays clearly showed he did, or that David O'Leary had fouled a defender. Again, there was no evidence.

George's mantra of 'do as I say' was working well; we were carrying out his instructions to the letter and now we were only one goal away from a shock win.

For the next half an hour, both sides slugged it out; Michael Thomas missed a decent chance for us but Ian Rush had gone off with a hamstring injury after 32 minutes and Liverpool were therefore shorn of their best attacking player and most lethal finisher. As the minutes ticked away it looked as if we were going to fail gallantly. All we needed was one more goal.

Then with one minute remaining of time added on for injuries, John Lukic had the ball in his hands and the ref was looking at his watch. Any second now he was going to blow for full time. Instead of thumping the ball down the pitch and hoping something might open up, our goalkeeper threw the ball to me. 'Don't give it to Dixon,' the manager is alleged to have said from the dugout. I got the ball out from under my feet and aimed for the reliable Smith whose velvet touch, chesting the ball into Thomas's path, was perfect.

Thomas brushed aside a challenge and suddenly he was in, with only Bruce Grobbelaar to beat. Mr Laid-Back, we used to call Michael. Sometimes his easy-going attitude infuriated us but here he was on his own and with great precision and calmness he guided a right-foot shot past the goalkeeper and into the net. I can remember that sharp intake of breath, the sheer disbelief when it went in, although I didn't actually see it roll past Grobbelaar. 'How did that happen?' I said to myself before bursting into tears.

Even then, it was still not over. Liverpool pushed forward desperately, knowing they only needed one goal. There was just a brief fear they might get it, but Thomas – who else? – calmly controlled the ball in the goalmouth mud before passing back to the safe hands of Lukic. Seconds later, agonising seconds later, Mr Hutchinson called time and the celebrations began. Liverpool's dejected players slumped to the floor; ours piled into each other delirious with delight and shock.

In fairness, Liverpool's horrified and shattered fans stayed behind to applaud us. To do so was a fine gesture. We had paid our respects to them beforehand, now they were paying theirs to us. To see your team deprived of a Double by a single goal must be hard to take, but they gave credit where credit was due and I shall always be grateful for their sportsmanship at such a dreadful time for so many families on Merseyside. Before the match there was a big wave of support for Liverpool all around the country after all they had been through in recent weeks. The neutral was definitely a Liverpool supporter that night. Yet we persevered and triumphed against the odds.

Liverpool had been expecting to win the title that night, so there were cases of champagne in the home dressing room in readiness to be popped. Kenny Dalglish kindly sent them to ours, another noble gesture in defeat. It was just as well he did because we had not anticipated victory, so we had not brought any alcohol with us, not so much as a solitary can of lager. As the coach headed back to London to a hastily arranged late-night session in a nightclub, one player stayed behind – me.

I had promised my mother I would head to Manchester after the match for a drink or two with an uncle who was home from Australia. Not expecting this superb result, I agreed in the days building up to the match and couldn't back out of it now. On the night Arsenal won their first league title for 18 years, I had two pints.

Two players stood out for me that night. The first was Thomas, the most annoyingly relaxed man on the planet. Nothing worried him ever. So when the ball fell to him, one on one with the goalkeeper, I knew he would go and score. I just knew it. If ever you had to choose a man to score from that position, it would have been him. He had scored a similar goal at Highbury earlier in the season and here he was, collected enough to wait for the goalkeeper to commit himself before shooting.

The other was David Rocastle. Lined up behind him every week I saw at first hand all his work, unseen by others more removed. George liked his midfield to protect his back four. 'I want my defenders to go on for ever,' he used to say. As we did. I was 38 when I retired, Nigel and Bouldy the same and Tony Adams 35. The midfield did protect us.

I will always remember Rocky for his hard work and his tirelessness but there was more to his game than that and he should have played many more times than he did for England. Then came his injuries and his illness and finally his premature death. It was all so sad. But we did later dedicate our 1989 win to Rocky – and to the 96 fans who lost their lives at Hillsborough. When I first moved down from Stoke, Rocky came with me to look at some furniture at World of Leather and, although I didn't buy anything, I thought it a lovely thing to do to help me get settled.

I don't think the Liverpool players much enjoyed our triumph and I can appreciate why. I did try to bring up the subject years later with Barnes but understandably he walked away. Two late incidents might haunt them even now. Barnes centred into the arms of Lukic in the dying seconds when he might more pragmatically have taken the ball into the corner flag and Aldridge had the chance to block Lukic's throw-out (illegally) to waste time, but having raised his arm initially, he put it down again. On little incidents like that a title was won and lost.

Years down the line, we made the documentary *89* and I must have watched it 60 times, often on a laptop on a plane, and I never cease to be thrilled by it. I still think Mickey Thomas is going to miss it. 'Shoot, Mickey, shoot.'

CHARLIE NICHOLAS

Charlie Nicholas
Forward
1983–1988

'Champagne Charlie' Nicholas was regarded as one of the most exciting talents in British football when he snubbed some of Europe's biggest clubs to join Arsenal from Celtic in the summer of 1983 after helping his boyhood heroes to back-to-back Scottish titles. The £750,000 fee made the party-loving Glaswegian the second most expensive import to move from north of the border. By his own admission, Nicholas struggled to adapt to Arsenal's direct style of play but his unique skills and maverick personality still endeared him to Gunners fans, who had been starved of success in the early 1980s. By the time he headed back to Scotland bound for Aberdeen in 1988, Nicholas had managed a respectable 34 goals in 151 league games during five typically flamboyant years at Highbury and also netted twice against Liverpool in the 1987 League Cup Final to end Arsenal's eight-year trophy drought. But it was his heroics in one north London derby in particular that truly made the Scotland international a terrace darling.

Tottenham 2–4 Arsenal

Division One
Monday, 26 December 1983
White Hart Lane, London
Attendance: 38,756

Tottenham	Arsenal
Clemence	Jennings
Hughton	Hill
Roberts	O'Leary
Perryman	Caton
Stevens	Sansom
Ardiles	Davis
Dick	Robson
Hoddle	Allinson
Cooke	Meade
Archibald	Nicholas
Brazil	Woodcock

Managers

Keith Burkinshaw	Don Howe

Goals

Archibald	Meade (2)
Roberts	Nicholas (2)

There are a lot of areas where Arsenal fans can claim I let them down and I would have to hold my hands up and agree, but when it came to facing Tottenham I was rarely found wanting.

I look at the number of goals great players like Ian Wright, Thierry Henry and Dennis Bergkamp, who was my personal favourite, scored and my stats in the north London derby would not be too far off theirs. In fact, I do not remember losing many matches against our fiercest foes; maybe only a couple.

Throughout my career there was always something about the really big occasions that seemed to bring the best out of me. I don't know whether it was about reputation or a personal agenda against the opposition to prove you were better than a particular player. I have never fully worked it out.

All I know is that in the build-up to what I viewed as a big game I would be more controlled with my training and would put a bit extra in to be fully mentally prepared for it. These were the games where players had to turn up and say: 'This is where I belong. This is what you bought me for.'

If you do not embrace that, then it will pass you by and you have got to turn up in these games because the essence of being a footballer for me was always about how the fans perceived you and what they thought of you. Some might love you, some might hate you, some might love your style and some may hate it, but if you can give them something back, that is why you are there.

As a Celtic fan I loved players who were trying to impress the crowd and that is what I wanted to do. I wanted to show them how hard I was trying to give them everything I had, not just by running about a lot but to try and get on the ball and make something happen.

I joined Arsenal in the summer of 1983 and there was certainly no shortage of clubs who were chasing me. I was playing for Scotland with 'King' Kenny Dalglish, Alan Hansen and Graeme Souness, who were the best in the world at the time, and they were encouraging me wholeheartedly to join Liverpool.

It made sense for that to be my number one choice because Liverpool played football the same way Celtic did and, being honest, that is where I should have gone as I would have won about 13 more medals!

But they had Ian Rush and Dalglish, so how the hell was I going to get in the team? I was 21, I'd had three years playing in Europe and playing every week with Celtic so I did not want to sit on the bench and just be a bit-part player.

My second option was Manchester United and I met Ron Atkinson, but was not particularly impressed by him and his self-indulgence, so I walked away from that one.

I also had interest from Inter Milan, which was teasing and tormenting me because I'd always had a desire to play in Europe but felt I was too young and naive at the time. Tottenham were trying to sell Steve Archibald or Garth Crooks to make way for me but I was not that convinced by them either, even though I did like Bill Nicholson.

Terry Neill was a nice, easy-going man, but I was really impressed with Don Howe, who had a great knowledge of the game and a lovely way about him. Whenever he spoke about the club he would say 'The Arsenal', and that stuck in my head.

Terry was a happy-go-lucky Irishman, but he had an issue in that, unlike Don, he was not seen as a leader in the dressing room and there was no real authority there. I am not sure either the fans or the players were ever that comfortable with Terry being the manager and even when he was sacked, I am not sure he was that bothered.

I remember on my first day, I called him Gaffer and the other players gave me a telling off, saying, 'His name is Terry or Tel, don't call him Gaffer.' I had just left Jock Stein and Billy

McNeill, two gods of the game, and there was no way I ever dared to call them by their first names because you had to show them respect.

Terry's football philosophy did not really suit mine either. He was more about defending and winning 1-0, but in that case, he should have bought someone other than me. Gradually Don changed that a little bit and he started playing me as a number ten, which is when I started to have an appreciation of how Don saw things. He still played the long ball, but the difference was that when it went up to the two strikers ahead of me I was able to support them while still facing the goal. That was much better for me, but Terry just never saw that.

Even before he became manager, Don was the general and he did most of the coaching. He was also the one who kept leading me towards Arsenal when I was deciding my future and I was excited by what they were trying to do in the transfer market. Their main targets were Liam Brady, who had become a bit homesick in Italy, so Arsenal had spoken to him about returning, and Ray Wilkins, who was having some financial issues with Chelsea. I also loved the red-and-white shirts from the days of Charlie George.

I think I confused everybody by picking Arsenal but it was really down to the picture Don had painted, what he was trying to teach me and where he was trying to take Arsenal. He said he wanted to make them a more attack-minded team, which, like the Brady and Wilkins signings, never really materialised, but he did enough to convince me.

I thought I could help make Arsenal great again and once I started to examine closely some of the players they already had, I could not believe how talented they were. There was Pat Jennings in goal, Kenny Sansom, the best left-back in the world, Graham Rix and his wand of a left-foot, David O'Leary, who was a glorious centre-back, and topped off up front with Tony

Woodcock, a European Cup winner with Nottingham Forest, who had also played in Germany.

Once I broke all that down, I thought to myself that this was not a bad team and did not need much adding to it if everything gelled together. That was when it became clear that Arsenal were the natural choice.

A lot of people said I only picked the move for the lifestyle, but I had lived in the goldfish bowl that was Glasgow for 21 years and for three years I was like their answer to David Beckham. I was followed everywhere by the press and was the topic of everyone's conversation, for good and bad reasons. I had an earring, wore designer gear and the public seemed to love the image, but I did not work on it or plan it. It just happened.

I had only ever been to London once before and that was when England battered Scotland 5-1, so it was not a happy memory. When I first arrived, I could not believe how big the place was. I was in digs near where David Dein and Tony Woodcock lived and when I would try and round people up for a pint after a game some of the lads said they lived an hour-and-a-half drive away.

That made team bonding very difficult. It was crazy and I think that was one of the factors as to why we did not gel. Liverpool were the best team in the world for a reason: they had great players but also a great team spirit and all used to go out together as mates. We never had that.

I was invited to many different parties and went to as many of them as I could, but the difference between London and Glasgow was that if the press were there, they would take a couple of snaps and then leave you alone – unless you were George Best, that is.

It was at those parties that I got to know George very well. I have met a lot of famous people but had never before been friends with a world star who caused so much fascination. People would just stand and stare, but be too frightened to come over and have a conversation with him.

Bestie loved football and loved footballers and was great pals with Frank McLintock. He had his issues in life, like all of us, and yes, he liked his drink and loved being a single man, but he was also the most shy and humble guy you could ever wish to meet.

I remember once with Arsenal we played in a small tournament in Cyprus. There was Paul Mariner, who was a wonderful person, Rixxy, Kenny Sansom, Tony Woodcock and me. George and Kevin Keegan were playing for a celebrity 11, but the two of them did not really get on and did not speak so, one afternoon, George called up to my hotel room to say he was at the bar with Kevin and wanted somebody to keep him company. I came down and told him the rest of the boys would join us later and he said: 'Do you mind if it's only two or three?' That is how shy he was.

By the time I pitched up at Arsenal, the Scottish press had already bestowed my 'Champagne Charlie' nickname upon me. That all came about because I said in an interview that I did not really drink beer and that I preferred wine.

They did not believe me and said I must have meant champagne so the headlines at first were 'Charlie Bubbles' before they cottoned on and changed it to 'Champagne Charlie'. I was on £30-a-week at Celtic and was paying my mum £10 of that, so I could not afford to drink champagne and it was only when I got to London that I started to embrace it because I was on a good salary and living well.

I do not have a lot of vanity and if people have an opinion of you, that is their right, so I was never in denial of it. Did I like it? Yes, at times. I still get called it now, even by my own family and my fellow Soccer Saturday pundits, and find it easier to accept than I did as a player because there were moments, especially when things were not going so well on the pitch, that I saw it as a dig at me.

I made my Arsenal debut on the opening day of the season in a 2-1 win against Luton, but did not play that well, which may have been down to letting the occasion get the better of me.

I have never been the nervous type and if I did get butterflies before a big game that was just about wanting to get on the ball and wanting to impress people, but this was different. I never really wanted to leave Celtic but they had pushed me out of the door because they wanted the big transfer fee, so I got it into my head that I needed to impress to prove I was worth the money.

My second game was against Wolves at Molineux and I played really well that day, scoring both goals in another 2-1 victory. My feeling as I was sitting on the team bus afterwards was one of relief, because I knew I had to get some goals early in my Arsenal career.

I always knew Tony Woodcock would get more goals than me because I was sacrificing my game a little bit to link up the play. As I have already mentioned, we were a bit of a long ball team and that was difficult for me to adapt to and I could not find the back of the net at Highbury for love nor money.

By the time the Boxing Day trip to White Hart Lane came around I had still only scored those two goals and was struggling. The ball was continually being bombed over the top of my head and I was in a bit of pain trying to work out how to adjust, because Arsenal could not change their style just to accommodate me, which I understood.

Thankfully, it all clicked for me on that afternoon when I came away with my two biggest Arsenal goals to that point in a 4-2 away victory.

My first goal was a precise shot into the corner from the edge of the penalty area and for my second I dinked the ball over the advancing Ray Clemence. That was a sweet moment as it happened right in front of the Arsenal fans behind the goal. It was also an unusual goal for how we used to play, because I ran from nowhere into the space before picking up the ball from midfield. I loved goals like that.

Spurs had Glenn Hoddle, one of the best players I ever played against, and they were a nice football team, the type of which we quite liked to play against, which was maybe another reason why I always seemed to perform well in these fixtures.

Before arriving at Arsenal, I had played in many Rangers against Celtic matches and the Old Firm game is more of a war than a derby; if you are a player on the losing side, you have to go into lockdown. It really is that dramatic and I probably kicked more people in those matches than in the rest of my career put together. I enjoyed Arsenal versus Tottenham more as a contest and it was more personal for the players in terms of trying to put one over each other.

Another famous derby goal I recall was on a bumpy Highbury pitch. Tottenham had stepped up to try and play offside and I did a little shuffle to get beyond their defence. The goalkeeper came out and I went around him, but because of the tight angle I knew I could not get any pace on the shot so I just concentrated on trying to steer it into the goal. Paul Miller, who always used to try and kick me, raced back to attempt to clear it and, thankfully for me, he ran too far and left the ball behind him. He crashed into the net with the ball trickling in a couple of seconds later.

It was just one of those magical moments, because I was right in front of the North Bank with nowhere to go. There was this little lad of about 12 who was staring at me and practically crying. There were people going mad all around him but I could not take my eyes of this little guy. It was as if he was trying to hypnotise me.

That goal was typical of my feet and how I tried to glide past people, it was not about pace, it was about movement and balance. I did get lucky with the finish but it is better to be lucky than good.

My party trick back then was the nutmeg and I remember Ray Wilkins saying to me once on a night out: 'Charlie, you enjoy nutmegging people more than scoring a goal.' That was absolutely not true but I did become the nutmeg king because it was cheeky and you could wind players up. I liked the devilment of it. I did it once to Graeme Souness in Scotland training and he chased me for 20 minutes so he could kick me. He held me down once he had caught me and I had a serious bruise for a few days afterwards.

I was fascinated by those little improvisations when you were in a tight spot and have to work out a way to get out of it. My favourite European player of all-time was Johan Cruyff and his Cruyff turn. Where did that come from? How did he work on that? I spent weeks trying to recreate it.

Players like Frank Worthington, George Best and Stan Bowles were a dream to watch and I loved being regarded as a maverick and found it hard to concentrate on the basics. I had spent years passing to my left and to my right and did not get any better doing that so I had to work on other things: flicks, touches and how to angle the body from taking a kick to still be able to see a midfield runner and play him in.

I spent a lot of time in training trying to steer passes into Tony Woodcock's path because he was a great runner, really pacey but also a clinical finisher so he would score lots of goals from me setting him up.

Not every manager I played under appreciated my maverick side and I knew as soon as George Graham walked into the building that I was on the time clock. When he was manager at Millwall, George used to drink in my local pub in Muswell Hill and we would always have a chat over a pint.

He was a fellow Glasgow boy and one day he said to me: 'Why the hell did you pick Arsenal? They don't suit you at all.' I explained that Don Howe had told me they were going to change their style and bring in more build-up play and George said that could never happen at Arsenal. Three weeks later he got the job and I thought, 'Here we go!'

I did not dislike George, we just never clicked, but he was a very good coach and I could tell there was a structure coming in, that he had something about him and that Arsenal were going to be a force again. He went back to the old Arsenal with discipline at the back and working the back four every day. He never really showed much interest in the strikers, so very quickly I could tell he did not want to play the way I did.

I knew my days were numbered so all I could do was focus on trying to get one trophy in the bag, which we did by beating Liverpool in the 1987 League Cup Final, with me bagging another brace, ending Ian Rush's proud record of having never been on the losing side in a game in which he had scored.

We always knew Rush would probably score as it was virtually impossible to keep him quiet for 90 minutes, but when he did score I feared the worst. I had already hit the post from close distance when I got my first goal and after that I think our superior fitness levels came through. Liverpool were so used to winning, whereas this was our one opportunity and we were determined to seize it. I thought we earned the victory, even though my second goal took a massive deflection off Ronnie Whelan to take it past Bruce Grobbelaar.

I knew Arsenal were a big club but only realised just how big when 150,000 people lined the streets of Islington for the open-top bus tour which followed that final. They were all locals and it was like nothing I had witnessed during my time in Glasgow.

I was bought to win trophies so at least I could say I had helped deliver that first one and then it was up to the rest of the players to move it on to the levels they did. But I think that final was the day things started to turn for the club.

I knew George had a serious chance of success because of the incredible young players ready to come through, including Tony

Adams, who was different class and had lots of fight and tenacity. David Rocastle was another and him and Paul Merson were the two really talented boys.

Rocky as a person was the most open, natural, smiley boy I had ever come across. I could not take my eyes off his gleaming teeth whenever he was talking. He really came to the fore when we beat Tottenham in the semi-final of our League Cup-winning campaign and he was unbelievable in the second leg at White Hart Lane. He went into his own world and was still wound up in the dressing room afterwards, still going like a Duracell battery and could not switch off.

As a Londoner himself, Rocky knew better than anyone that the derbies were vitally important, in my case for survival with the Arsenal fans as much as anything. That is why the goals I scored on that first December afternoon meant so much to me, because it was a turning point for the team and for me. It was also my way of saying to the supporters 'If you stay patient with me, hopefully I can produce a bit more for you', which they did. The only problem was it happened away from home and not at Highbury – again.

CHARLIE GEORGE

Charlie George
Forward
1968–1975

Charlie George was born in Islington, deep in Arsenal territory, and raised in nearby Holloway. As a youngster he watched the Gunners from the North Bank, dreaming of the chance to wear the famous red and white. This he achieved when he was taken on as an apprentice at the age of 16, breaking into the first team two years later. Famous for his long, dark hair and mercurial forward talent, George was part of the Gunners team which won the Inter-Cities Fairs Cup in 1970 when he was 19 and the League and FA Cup Double a year later. George became the 'Darling of the North Bank' and seemed to be on the threshold of greatness. But he fell out with disciplinarian manager Bertie Mee and was sold to Derby for a knock-down £100,000 in 1975 when he was still to reach his prime. Scandalously, George earned only one England cap (and that for about an hour) before some furious comments aimed at national boss Don Revie ended his international career before it had begun. He is secure in Arsenal folklore for his goal – the extra-time winner – against Liverpool in the FA Cup Final of 1971. Flat on his back, arms aloft, the image of George in the immediate aftermath of his glorious moment is one of football's most iconic. Later, George was a constantly moving figure with Minnesota Kicks, Southampton, Nottingham Forest, Bulova of Hong Kong, Bournemouth, Dundee United and Coventry among some but not all of his clubs. But it is with Arsenal that he will always be associated. The match of Charlie's life was not the cup final, as might be supposed, but the fifth-round tie at Maine Road in the same year. George later ran a pub in Hampshire and now regales Gunners fans in the hospitality area at the Emirates Stadium with some wonderful tales of football's golden era.

Manchester City 1-2 Arsenal

FA Cup fifth round
Wednesday, 17 February 1971
Maine Road, Manchester
Attendance: 45,105

Manchester City	Arsenal
Corrigan	Wilson
Book	Rice
Mann	McNab
Doyle	Storey
Booth	McLintock
Oakes	Simpson
Heslop	Armstrong
Bell	Kennedy
Lee	Sammels
Young	George
Bowyer	Radford

Managers
Malcolm Allison	Bertie Mee

Goals
Bell	George (2)

I was lucky even to have taken part in that FA Cup Final against Liverpool. In the first game of the 1970/71 season I suffered a double fracture of a leg at Everton when I ran into their goalkeeper, Gordon West, an injury so bad that I was told I might never play again. So, as the season slowly gathered momentum in league and cup, I had to watch the first half of it from the stands. It was not until the New Year that I was able to play again and in fact missed the third-round victory at non-league Yeovil in early January because I was still making my way back. Eventually I was fit again and at just the right time. I played 17 of the remaining league games and scored five goals, but it was in the cup that I was able to make the biggest impression. I scored in the fourth, fifth and sixth rounds and then, of course, the final, but we didn't do it the easy way. To win the cup we had to play in nine matches. Add those to 42 in the league and decent runs in the League Cup and the Inter-Cities Fairs Cup, and it proved to be a long and arduous season.

After beating Yeovil 3-0 we were drawn to play Portsmouth, a division below us, at Fratton Park. Driven by a large and passionate crowd, Pompey pushed us all the way and we needed a Peter Storey penalty to earn us a replay after a 1-1 draw. I was a sub that day but started the second match and again we had to work hard to win 3-2. I got our second goal and the reward was a trip to Manchester City and a tie I'll never forget.

City had some superb players like Francis Lee, Colin Bell, Mike Summerbee, Mike Doyle and the goalkeeper Joe Corrigan. You could go through the whole line-up and see nothing but top quality, and the management team of Joe Mercer and Malcolm Allison had helped establish them as one of the country's top clubs. In front of a full-house at Maine Road it was going to be one of the toughest matches of our season.

What I liked about it was the mud. Lots of it all over the pitch. Don't ask me why but I loved playing when the conditions were at their most difficult. You can forget about the superb flat, green surfaces of today. I liked mud and for some reason was at my best when there were pools of water and you could hear the squelching underfoot as you ran. Being Manchester, it poured with rain for days. The original match on the Saturday was postponed because it was so wet and it was only just about playable when we went up there on the Wednesday. I loved playing at Maine Road, long since replaced by the Etihad Stadium, and always played well there. It was a big open ground and my favourite, I think, of all the grounds I played at. Everything pointed to a good night for me ... a top stadium and plenty of mud.

But there was one incident which made it complete. The crowd was building up and we were in the dressing room before going out at the start. It's a nervous time and most players are lost in their own little worlds waiting to be called out. I was no different. Then Frank McLintock, our captain, came up to me and said he had just been speaking to the flamboyant City coach Malcolm Allison, a man renowned for his big cigar, fedora and provocative comments. 'Yes,' said Frank. 'He says you're crap.' In response I think I said something like 'no problem', but it clearly was. It got to me big time. I went out on to that pitch seething.

The surface soon cut up, players were slithering everywhere and the tension was incredible. I was desperate to prove a point to Allison, desperate to show he was wrong and, after about 15 minutes, my chance came. We got a free kick on the edge of the area and there was enough room for me to lash a right-foot shot beyond Corrigan's dive. One-nil to the Arsenal. I looked over at Allison in the dugout. No movement.

Midway through the second half Bob McNab played a pass down the left and I ran through from the halfway line unmarked to shoot past Corrigan. Fantastic. What a feeling. I ran back to the halfway line and collapsed on my back, arms raised in the way I later did against Liverpool in the final. I called it my Jesus pose.

I lay there waiting for my team-mates to catch up and join the celebrations. I don't know why I did it, but there are those who suggested I was wasting time deliberately. To be honest, I was just tired; I had run from the halfway line. I only ever brought out the Jesus pose twice in wild moments of extreme success and this one was aimed firmly at Malcolm Allison. As we gathered our composure for the restart, I looked over at Big Mal. Again, no movement.

Bell, one of the great players of my playing time, pulled a goal back for City but we held on against increasing pressure to complete a superb 2-1 win. At the final whistle there was only one man I wanted to see and I followed Allison up the tunnel. I gave him a volley of abuse, a torrent of swear words which made it clear that his view of me as 'crap' was way off the mark. I had made him eat his words. Baffled, Allison later saw Frank and asked him why I had behaved so furiously and singled him out for such personal abuse. 'What's up with Charlie?' he said. Frank replied: 'Oh, that's nothing. I told him you had said to me you thought he was crap to gee him up and it looks like it worked.'

Frank had been winding me up as he often did in an effort to get the best out of me. I needed it. Thanks to his masterful psychology, I produced one of my best performances and poor old Malcolm was the fall guy.

We stayed up overnight and the next day returned to London by train. Waiting for us when we arrived were Thames Television who said Eamonn Andrews, host of a nightly news programme, wanted to interview me about my heroics the night before. I said: 'Tell him to forget it. I'm going home.' Not many people snubbed the great Eamonn Andrews.

Later, we needed two matches to dispose of Leicester in the quarter-final and another two to see off Stoke in the semis. I scored in both and now we had to beat Liverpool to claim the

Double at the end of a long and demanding season. The rest is history. Steve Heighway put Liverpool ahead, Eddie Kelly equalised and the moment for which I'm always remembered came in the 111th minute. John Radford set me up with the pass and I belted a 20-yard right-foot shot past Ray Clemence. Out came the Jesus pose.

It certainly killed the game as it took precious minutes to restart and we hung on easily enough. I should have patented my goal celebrations and the Jesus pose was never repeated. I once said it was more important than Jesus because Jesus had never scored in a Wembley final. It was a joke, of course, not meaning to offend anyone. But one guy came up to me and said he was a Christian and would pray for me after my blasphemy.

That afternoon I was able to reflect on winning the FA Cup, the Football League and the Inter-Cities Fairs Cup all before I was 20. We had a great side and for the next year or two we competed strongly for all the major honours. There was a lot of competition in those days. Any one of four or five clubs could win the league and 10 or 12 could win the cup; not like now. Don Howe was a great coach and, while I'm not belittling what Bertie Mee did for the club, I didn't get on with him. He was the ex-physiotherapist who masterminded the Double and built a strong side but we fell out several times when he felt the need to discipline me. So when I left for Derby in 1975, where I had three great years on their muddy pitch, the wonderful team was breaking up and it was time to go. I had gone as far as I could with Arsenal.

I would have liked to have played more than once for England but I'm not moaning about it now, deep into retirement. There is nothing I can do to change what happened. Don Revie played me out of position against the Republic of Ireland in my only international and I didn't do myself any favours when I had a right go at him when he took me off.

Anyway, I'm back with the Gunners these days and I get the chance to see old team-mates and recount the tales of my past. Much as I enjoyed playing elsewhere, Arsenal were always my club.

NIGEL WINTERBURN

Nigel Winterburn
Defender
1987–2000

Nigel Winterburn had big boots to fill when he was signed by Arsenal from Wimbledon in 1987 as a future successor to another legendary left-back, Kenny Sansom. By his own admission, Winterburn struggled to make much of an impression in his early days at the club but would go on to prove a more than capable replacement for Sansom to earn his own place in Gunners folklore. By the time he left for West Ham aged 36, Winterburn had racked up 12 goals, the majority of them of the spectacular variety, and a mountain of assists in amongst a 584-match Arsenal career which also saw him lift seven major trophies. But it is the thrilling climax to the 1997/98 Premier League and FA Cup Double win in Arsene Wenger's first full season as manager, and a Marc Overmars-inspired win at Old Trafford in particular, that Winterburn remembers with most glee.

Manchester United 0-1 Arsenal

Premier League
Saturday, 14th March 1998
Old Trafford, Manchester
Attendance: 55,174

Manchester United	**Arsenal**
Schmeichel	Seaman
Curtis (Thornley)	Dixon
G Neville	Adams
Berg	Keown
Irwin	Winterburn
Beckham	Parlour (Garde)
Johnsen (May)	Petit
P Neville (Solskjaer)	Vieira
Scholes	Overmars
Sheringham	Bergkamp
Cole	Wreh (Anelka)

Managers

Sir Alex Ferguson   Arsene Wenger

Goal

Overmars

There are certain points in every season that you can look back on as being pivotal, and a last-minute goal or a crucial missed chance in a particularly critical match can so often be the thin dividing line between success and failure.

Walking off the pitch at Old Trafford as our jubilant travelling supporters, including THAT famous fan with the frizzy hair, celebrated high up in the stands was one such moment. The atmosphere in our dressing room after Marc Overmars had come up with his all-important late winner was electric. It was absolutely incredible, the like of which I had only witnessed previously in the aftermath of title-clinching victories or after winning a cup.

Looking around at my hyperactive team-mates, I could see the belief was there that we could now go on and achieve something quite spectacular. It was the victory that propelled us towards the most unlikely of league titles.

Some bookmakers had already paid out by then on United being crowned champions because we were 12 points behind at kick-off with games running out, but we never gave in. We knew, of course, that we would have to put a sensational run together and we did, not losing a single game from Christmas until we had secured an unmatchable lead at the top and conceding very few goals in the process.

We had already beaten United in the reverse fixture at Highbury, with David Platt's glancing near-post header from my corner earning us what turned out to be a precious 3-2 triumph in a real ding-dong battle, but the game at Old Trafford was so important for us. We went into it knowing we could not afford to lose, but realising we had the ability to win and, that if we did, then it would give us a major mental boost and put that doubt into the minds of United players that the tide was turning significantly.

The build-up to it was tense because we knew that if we lost, the title was gone. We were the better side throughout the 90 minutes but the ball just would not seem to go in, so it was a relief when Marc stroked in the winner 11 minutes from the end.

Marc had a sensational season, exemplified by his goal. The ball was slipped into our quicksilver Dutch winger on his favoured left-hand side and he flicked it on before showing great composure to roll it beyond the advancing Peter Schmeichel, who would later injure his hamstring whilst racing back to his own penalty area after coming up for a corner in desperate search of an equaliser.

I got on tremendously well with Marc and our connection on the pitch was sensational. I played my first game with him and from that point forward, I knew exactly what he wanted me to do with the ball when I was in possession in terms of where and how he wanted it played.

I did not really need to talk to him because I could tell what he was going to do from the body positions he took up and little knowing looks that he gave me. I knew whether he wanted the ball played into his feet or rolled slowly so he could turn it around the corner. Other times he would feint to come and get it and spin in behind so I would just have to chip it over the top for him.

To play with Marc was a real honour. The outlet he gave you with his pace, coupled with the ability he had, was incredible and he scored some important goals that year as well. From a defensive point of view, I just used to stick him in front of me. He didn't need to tackle and I would just tell him whether to pass the ball inside or outside.

Marc, who used to collect old toys as one of his hobbies, was a good guy in the dressing room and would come out and socialise with us, as did most of the overseas lads.

Arsene Wenger was big on diet and how to replenish your body after games and after training, but we were never told we could not have a beer. I think he trusted us that, although we'd had a drinking culture at the club, we would not abuse the system any more.

I remember many times playing abroad in pre-season when we would go for a stroll in the evening and have a few pints of beer. We would be going off and looking to have a drink while the French lads were all about coffee and there were definitely a couple of them who used to have it with a secret cigarette when Arsene was not around.

That was the different culture of the two sets of players. They did things slightly differently; it was never a problem, although I don't think they could quite believe how much we drunk to start with.

Marc was not the only Dutchman in our line-up. We also had Dennis Bergkamp, the best player I ever played with. I enjoyed playing with a lot of my team-mates, but he is the one that stands out because his ability was sensational and he portrayed himself with a calmness that suggested everything was under control. He also had great vision coupled with incredible awareness and some of the goals he scored were remarkable. He was a joy to play with and to watch.

There is always a lot of debate and I would not have a dispute with anybody who put Thierry Henry above Dennis as Arsenal's greatest modern superstar, but I only spent a year with Thierry and at that time he was not the sensational player he would grow to become.

Dennis also had a great mentality, because it did not happen for him straight away and he took a bit of time to adapt to the English game after his arrival from Inter Milan, but the quality was always there and I realised very quickly from training with him that he was going to be a special player for the club for a number of years. As a nation we can be a bit quick to write off players without giving them the chance to settle, particularly those from a different country, but at times you have to find your own way to make sure you are as good as you expect yourself to be and Dennis definitely did that to become a real fans' favourite.

His fear of flying has been well documented, but we never overly worried about it. If we were playing in Europe, somewhere he could not get to by other means in a reasonable amount of time, then we accepted he was not going to play. None of his team-mates ever criticised him for that even though we all knew we were a better team with him in it.

Dennis and Marc were just two of a number of great characters we had in a squad blessed with talent as well as mental toughness.

Tony Adams summed it all up with the famous volley he scored against Everton in the 4-0 win at Highbury that confirmed us as champions, before raising both arms in the air in celebration. I always felt that photo should have had a bubble coming out of his mouth with the caption: 'I told you I was Mr Arsenal.' Tony was such an iconic player for the club, so strong and resilient with what he had gone through off the pitch and managing to change his life around along the way.

Then there was Ian Wright, who was a complete pain in the backside. He was always so hyper before matches, especially in the last 15 minutes prior to kick-off when I wanted to be focused and needed somewhere quiet to sit and figure out what I wanted to do and who I was playing against. He was hyper beyond belief, but it was not a show, that is how he is: so bubbly and infectious.

The mix was incredible because we had players that were quite reserved and others who were right out there and in your face. I loved Wrighty, but at times I wanted to say, 'Just sit down and be quiet.' He was just a bundle of energy and that is exactly how he played; he did not hold back on or off the pitch.

I know George Graham says in this book that we should have won a European Cup under Arsene and I do not disagree that we should have fared a lot better in Europe than we did. It is the one thing you can say we failed at and we did let ourselves down in the big European competitions.

The season after winning the Double we decided to play our Champions League games at Wembley and that was a disaster! I never understood why we did it and still don't. Why would you move away from Highbury with its small, intense atmosphere where night games were sensational? Wembley was a great facility with big open spaces and I know the idea was to try and let more supporters in but we lost so much in terms of home advantage.

The other reason the Premier League and FA Cup Double was extra special for me is because I was 35 and you always hear these little whispers from people writing you off. That became a challenge to show that they had underestimated me, based on my age and not my ability on the pitch.

When Arsene came there were rumours flying around that he had been told the back four were too old and that he needed to try and mix that up a little bit if he wanted to create a successful team.

I loved his training sessions and the different methods and different intensity Arsene brought, particularly in his first pre-season, which was before the Double-winning campaign. The different thought level he put into it made me realise it was something I wanted to be part of and I really had to push hard to make sure I convinced the manager I was what he needed in his team.

In my early days a lot of people would say I was not a great trainer but, as the years went on, I certainly trained harder because the younger guys coming through pushed me so hard. That enabled me to carry on playing until I was nearly 40.

I had a drive and desire to prove people wrong and thankfully for me and the whole of the back four, Arsene had the insight to look at our performances and not the age of the individual players.

The make-up of our defence had changed slightly from our previous title wins in 1989 and 1991, because Martin Keown had replaced Steve Bould as the mainstay alongside Tony in the centre.

Martin had been at the club before I arrived, left and then came back so we knew his quality. He was so intense and never gave opponents an easy time. He had good pace, was a terrific player and was not scared to pick a fight with anybody.

On the day of this Old Trafford victory, United had David Beckham on the right wing and that was always an interesting duel because, although his quality was in his passing and crossing, the spaces he took up on the pitch made it very difficult for a left-back to mark him. He very rarely came directly up against you and would often let Gary Neville run on and drop into midfield from where he could pop up and spray passes around. He was a very clever player.

You can always look back at other matches that season as key turning points and people will identify with my long-range screamer at Chelsea just because it came so late in the game to give us another 3-2 victory in a brilliant derby match.

Most people talk about the Chelsea goal because it was vital, but my favourite Arsenal goal was the one I scored against Wimbledon towards the end of the 1988/89 season. The main reason it stands out is because it was from long range – with my RIGHT foot. I think that surprised a lot of people, including me. We were playing with the old Adidas Tango ball and it just flew like an arrow into the top corner, never deviating from its path.

I don't really have any disappointments from my career, but I wish I could have made just one start for England in addition to a couple of sub appearances to show people that I was good enough to be in and around the squad a lot more than I was.

It didn't happen because there were some good players at other clubs and from very early on in my Arsenal career, I did not bother to look at England squads when they were announced. I knew deep down inside that I was not going to be part of them.

I do not know why I was not selected; certain managers just thought other players were better suited than me. In the end, although it was hard to take, I just got on with it and focused on my club football.

Rio Ferdinand always talks about the clique culture of the England squad and trying to integrate into that environment when you have played against one of the big teams the week before then have to go and be mates with those same opponents on international duty.

I have to admit that the couple of times I did get into squads I found that side of things quite difficult and was not completely confident with what was going on, so in that sense it was a bit of a relief not to be part of it. Maybe it had its advantages in the long run.

Another of Arsene's biggest strengths was that he was very calm and calculated, particularly during matches, and I never knew him get upset or go overboard with the celebrations. On a lot of occasions, he did not even come into the dressing room straight away at half-time. He used to stand outside and let the players have their say amongst themselves and sometimes, when things were going badly, there would be a bit of arguing and shouting between us. As soon as he stepped into the room, everybody sat down and shut up and he would point out where we had been going wrong and how we could pull a result out of the bag in the second half.

It was really weird being sat there waiting for a manager to tear into you and then he comes in and does not say a word. In the whole time I played under him I never heard Arsene raise his voice and even remember once he chucked his assistant Pat Rice out of the dressing room because he was having a go at some of the lads.

He showed emotion when we won and would come in with a smiley face, but always seemed to have his feelings under control even in the face of provocation.

Alex Ferguson was the master of mind games, but Arsene was not going to have any of that and was not afraid to speak his mind. He must have been a journalist's dream in that respect and the way he responded to Ferguson's comments made me chuckle a few times.

The rivalry between the two managers was interesting to watch and was great to be part of because there was a real battle for supremacy going on between the two teams for a few seasons but Arsene never let the rivalry interfere with his preparation for games. We all knew it was there and that it riled him a little bit but he was big enough to handle it.

I have always said the 1997/98 team is the best I have played in in terms of flair and ability and that is with no disrespect to the players I played with under George Graham.

If you looked at the players we had in 89 and 91 and the unfancied teams a lot of us had been signed from, I do not think any supporter outside Arsenal would have put our squad in the top three in the country. We had real quality players whose reputations grew as the years went on, but the difference with the 98 team was that we could see the quality that was coming into the club and had the feeling it would be a special period.

The style of play and the freedom that Arsene Wenger gave us made it feel like we were just going out to have a Sunday afternoon kickabout in the park and that is what gave me so much enjoyment. I have so much admiration and pride for the other teams I played in because that was the process that allowed Arsene to come in and start to reconstruct and change the way the club was moving forward. There is no question in my mind that George built the foundations for him to take over.

It was George who brought me to the club and there was no doubt from the moment I walked into the marble halls that I was going to sign. As soon as I stepped in there, I loved everything about it, but my first six months as an Arsenal player spent mainly playing in the reserves were horrible.

At Wimbledon I had the reputation of being a regular starter and had won Player of the Year for four years running, so maybe

I got away with stuff in training that I could not any more. I had to turn that around and push myself really hard.

I had real doubts, because I was used to playing at Plough Lane in front of 6,000 people and walking out at kick-off with the three points meaning so much to the team. That excitement brought me alive and then all of a sudden you go to Arsenal, a big club with great history, and are walking out at Highbury for the reserves in front of about 100 people. I felt as flat as a pancake and questioned myself several times as to whether I had made the right decision.

Kenny Sansom was still there and he was someone I used to really admire and watch and learn from in training, but also in games I used to study what he was doing and how he coped with certain situations.

Kenny's presence meant for a while that whenever I did get the opportunity to play for the first team it was mostly at right-back, but my motivational tool throughout my career came from when I was a youngster at Birmingham and Ron Saunders decided I wasn't good enough.

I joined Birmingham straight from school and had earned rave reviews and was being told I was going to make it, so it was a shock to find myself out of the club in double-quick time. I used to remember that experience of standing in Ron's office and the dejection I felt every time any doubts crept in to my mind later in my career. I just looked back on that feeling and kept it in the pit of my stomach.

I knew no matter what happened to me it would never be that bad again and that was my driving force, even in games when I was playing poorly and needed to lift myself. I just wanted to show certain people they had made a huge mistake.

I did allow myself a little smile every time I went up to lift a trophy or after a big victory and that wonderful afternoon at Old Trafford would have been no different. Thanks Ron.

RAY PARLOUR

Ray Parlour
Midfielder
1992–2004

Ray Parlour was one of a number of players who came through Arsenal's prolific youth academy under the expert tutelage of Pat Rice. The Essex-born midfielder made his first-team debut against Liverpool in January 1992 and went on to play more than 300 league games for the Gunners. Affectionately known as 'the Romford Pele', Parlour was an industrious cog in the Arsenal team that won the FA Cup and League Cup Double under George Graham in 1993 and the European Cup Winners' Cup a year later. It was under Arsene Wenger that Parlour says he played the best football of his career and blossomed into a full England international, cruelly robbed of a place in Kevin Keegan's squad for Euro 2000 because of a knee injury. Under Wenger, Parlour added three Premier League titles and two more FA Cups to his list of honours, each celebrated with his usual enthusiasm and the consumption of several pints of lager. Parlour was also one of the Invincibles who went 49 games unbeaten. After leaving Arsenal, Parlour continued his career at Middlesbrough and Hull before retiring in 2007 to become a much-loved presenter on talkSPORT, where his breakfast show partnership with Alan Brazil (and the pair's drinking antics) became legendary. He is also an ambassador for Arsenal and a regular in their former-players' team.

Manchester United 0-1 Arsenal

Premier League
Tuesday, 8 May 2002
Old Trafford, Manchester
Attendance: 67,580

Manchester United	Arsenal
Barthez	Seaman
P Neville	Lauren
Blanc	Keown
Brown	Campbell
Silvestre	Cole
Scholes	Ljungberg
Keane	Parlour
Veron (van Nistelrooy)	Vieira
Giggs	Edu
Solskjaer	Wiltord
Forlan (Fortune)	Kanu (Dixon)

Managers
Sir Alex Ferguson — Arsene Wenger

Goal
Wiltord

I was lucky enough to win nine major trophies and go a whole season unbeaten during my Arsenal career, but there is one week in May 2002 that I cherish above all others. In the space of just four days I managed to score in the FA Cup at the Millennium Stadium and then win man of the match at Old Trafford as we clinched the Premier League title to complete my second Double. Life as a footballer does not get any better than that.

We got the first trophy in the bag by beating Chelsea in Cardiff on the Saturday. That was a really tight, tough game that could have gone either way and we were getting tired towards the end when I managed to pick out the top corner to open the scoring with 20 minutes left.

Chelsea had created a few decent chances by then and David Seaman made a couple of good saves to keep them out. Every team needs a top goalkeeper behind them and we definitely had that, even if Dave took a bit of stick for his hairstyle. One day we all went out to training wearing fake ponytails. Dave saw the funny side and let out one of his big laughs.

We used to do a few pranks like going up to someone from behind and pulling their shorts down and I got caught out by that joke when Dennis Bergkamp did it to me during a pre-season game in front of a packed stand. Football cannot be serious all the time and we knew how to have a bit of a giggle.

The move for my goal against Chelsea started when Sylvain Wiltord picked up the ball in midfield and I made a run from deep. The Chelsea players seemed to keep backing off in front of me until eventually I ended up facing Marcel Desailly so I decided to use his body as a shield. He turned his back on the ball, which you should never do as a defender, and I bent my shot towards goal. On another day it might have hit the crossbar or the goalkeeper, Carlo Cudicini in this case, would have got his fingertips to it, but luckily enough this time around the ball flew into the net.

I did that type of thing a lot in training, but to do it in the FA Cup Final was a bit different and we always knew the first goal would be crucial because if Chelsea had scored first, I don't think we would have got back into it.

Freddie Ljungberg sealed the win by becoming the first man in 40 years to score in successive FA Cup finals with another lovely strike. Freddie was a great lad, but he used to wear some dodgy clothes, big chains and jeans that were too small for him. He thought that was fashion but we would hang his stuff up in the middle of the changing room for a laugh, not that it stopped him wearing it.

I was always going to celebrate scoring in the cup final as that does not happen every day, so I had a few beers after the game. Arsene Wenger stopped me from drinking on the plane on our way home because we still had the league match to come a few days later, but I went to my favourite Indian restaurant when we landed and made up for it there.

We left Cardiff on the Saturday night, did a light training session the next day and a full session on the Monday before travelling to Manchester on Tuesday morning, the day of the match. We knew exactly what was at stake but tried to treat it as a normal game, because otherwise the pressure can build on you and that is when you play poorly.

We were on a high anyway from winning the cup and just found that little bit extra from somewhere, which we did not think we had in our bodies, but we did.

That was the beauty of trying to win trophies and I tended to find big matches like this one would take care of themselves. It was the same in the FA Cup, where the hardest part was always the third round and playing away at somewhere like Carlisle. Our visit was their final and if you were not up for it and dropped your level a little bit that is when shocks happened.

You always had to be focused on every game and to make sure that even if you had a poor day you did enough for the players around you, like winning the ball back, to make sure you got the job done.

We had a tremendous will to win, which was a massive asset because if we played badly, we would usually end up getting a draw due to our fighting spirit. That is the attitude that we had even in training and nobody wanted to lose a five-a-side or an eight versus eight. Sometimes Arsene would have to step in and tell us to mind the tackles because the challenges were flying in. That is just how committed we all were to the cause.

United had the benefit of having the extra rest and it had been a long, hard season for us, but the performance itself was fantastic from every single player. We gave everything that we had left, which was not loads on the back of the cup final.

We were also without Dennis Bergkamp and Thierry Henry that day, two of the best foreign imports the Premier League has ever seen and two of our key men. Nwankwo Kanu and Wiltord played up front and it shows how strong the squad we had back then was that, even without Bergkamp and Henry, we had two superb players like that to come into the side.

Kanu was very laid back, but a quality player and you never tried to kick him in training because he had the ability to turn you inside out. He had size 14 feet but could control a ball like you would never believe, a great first touch, and was just a very talented player. He was a real asset and Sylvain was underrated as well. He was a very fit lad who would run everywhere when he came off the bench and was also technically very good. They were guys who did not always play on a regular basis but were so needed in winning trophies because if there were a couple of injures, you knew they could step up and do a job. You always need a bit of back up and you could not get two better players than them.

They never sulked either, because they knew it was a competitive position with Thierry and Dennis, but they were pleased to play their part.

We had a very good side, with Patrick Vieira, Edu and Freddie controlling the midfield. I was a little bit older than Patrick but could tell as soon as he came into the club what a top player he was, just from the way he acted and conducted himself. Nothing ever fazed Patrick; he always wanted the ball and had that big, physical presence as well. We always seemed to link up well, whether I was playing out on the wing or in the middle. He was a dream player to play with because he had that competitive edge and never gave up.

Patrick's battles with Roy Keane became infamous and, whenever people ask me who was the best player I faced, Roy's name always comes into my mind. He was fantastic for United and when the going got tough you knew people like Roy Keane would stand up. Their midfield around that time was very special: Ryan Giggs on the left, David Beckham on the right and Paul Scholes and Keane in the middle. We always knew that area of the pitch would be important to determine which team came out on top.

Patrick and Roy were both winners who wanted to win every game and every challenge and that is why sometimes it went a little bit over the top like when they clashed in the tunnel at Highbury. When you have 11 players who all want to win, spats like that can happen, but that is part of being a successful team and everybody always shook hands at the end of the game because you knew you were playing for your shirt and for your team-mates.

Arsene recruited a lot in France and we had a good blend of British and foreign players. The foreign boys made us better players with their professionalism, which rubbed off on the rest of us. We still used to go out and have fun as a team and had group meals every now and again. They did not drink as much as the British lads but still had a glass of wine and we enjoyed everyone's different cultures. We all got on very well and all respected each other because we all wanted success together.

Football is a team game first and foremost and you need good players around you, but the man of the match award from this particular game is one I am proud of because that was no small achievement given how many great players there were on the pitch.

United were the team to beat during that era and they dominated the early 1990s which meant, if you could beat them, you had a really good chance of winning the league. Things changed a bit when Roman Abramovich came in at Chelsea, but in the late 90s and early 2000s there was a massive rivalry between our two clubs and it was always either us or United who seemed to be lifting the championship trophy come the end of the season.

Even in our Invincible season a few years later, Ruud van Nistelrooy missed a penalty against us which, if he had scored as he usually did, would have taken away our unbeaten record and denied us a bit of history.

It was the same when United won their famous treble in 1999. Dennis missed a penalty in the FA Cup semi-final against them at Villa Park, which we went on to lose in extra time, and we were beaten 1-0 at Leeds in our penultimate game of the season when a 0-0 draw would have probably seen us win the league again. From going for another Double, we suddenly ended the season trophy-less and that illustrates how much of a fine line it was between both sides.

The two teams drove each other on and at the start of every season when the fixtures were released in the summer, we would always look for when we were playing United as that was our biggest game and, if we could get four points off them, we considered that a very good return and knew it should be enough to win the league.

They were always fantastic games against United and we suffered our share of defeats, as they did, but they were great matches to play in because you always felt, coming off the pitch, that you had been involved in a proper game.

My brother was in the crowd the night we won the title and he says it was one of the best games I ever played, given the circumstances of going for the championship against one of the best teams in the country who were so determined to stop us doing it in their own backyard.

Obviously, it is a nice feeling to win the league at home in front of your own fans but doing it at one of your rivals is even better. We did it at Tottenham in 2004 and at Old Trafford on this night. As an Arsenal fan or player, you cannot pick two better places to do it.

We had happy memories of going to Old Trafford from four years earlier when Marc Overmars scored in a 1-0 victory; a goal which proved the catalyst for us going on to overturn a big points deficit and pip United to the title en route to winning my first Double in Arsene's first full season in charge.

That was a different season because we were so far behind, albeit with a few games in hand, but you would always rather have the points on the board. We managed to win ten games in a row, culminating in that memorable last game of the season at home to Everton when our captain Tony Adams scored his wonder goal.

Some of the older guys in the team like Adams, Lee Dixon and Steve Bould had experience of winning trophies but it was our first title as a group and my first title, which was important because the league table does not lie – the best team always finishes at the top and the worst at the bottom.

Tony was a great servant to Arsenal and a good friend but he stitched me up with George Graham when I first broke into the team as a 17-year-old. As part of my initiation I had to stand up and do a speech in front of everyone the night before we played Norwich and I did not have a clue what to say, so I asked Tony.

He advised me to make sure I mention something about the tank top the manager was wearing, which I did, not realising George was a little bit fragile about his clothes and did not like people taking the mickey out of them. George looked at me and snarled, 'I think you have said enough', and ordered me to sit down while all the other lads were sniggering. Thanks, Tony.

George was an excellent tactician and was defensively very solid. I continued that under Arsene Wenger in terms of tracking back and making sure I stayed in position, which was all down to George and the way he coached me. Arsene came in and I got a lot better technically because of what we did in training. If you can put both aspects together you end up with a decent player.

Apart from a brief spell with Bruce Rioch, who I got on well with but some players didn't, I played my entire Arsenal career under two managers and they both had very different styles. George was more of a ranter and would say what he thought after the game, whereas Arsene would assess the situation and have a meeting the next day in training and ask the players where they thought it went wrong, rather than address it straight away in the dressing room.

They were both very successful and both desperate to win. They both worked us every day in training to make sure we were ready for a match day, which, in my opinion, is the manager's main job – to make you prepared and get you ready so that once you cross that white line it is down to the players to know exactly what you have to do for the team and to do it.

I knew almost as soon as he arrived that Arsene was going to do very well at Arsenal. When we started training with him, you could tell he was focused and that he had his own ideas. Some of the players he brought in were superb and you could see he loved football; he could not wait to be in training every day to help people improve. He was the one who would put all the training drills on and I don't think he ever missed one single training session. He was always out on that field with you and even after training I could ask to do a bit extra and he would say, 'No problem.' He would not get one of the coaches, he would come and do it with you. That is the sort of guy he was.

Arsene told me when he was first appointed that he believed in me and that he just wanted me to go out and play. He said if I did well for him, I would be in the team the next week and he was very true to his word. As a player that is all you need to hear so I made sure I was putting in performances every week and, before I knew it, I was a regular for the next three or four seasons.

He was brilliant and George was very similar; he was always drilling people and working on that defensive unit. I am sure our back four would always say that George played a big part in their success and keeping clean sheets, which they were brilliant at.

Back to the United game, which we won 1-0 courtesy of a Wiltord goal 11 minutes into the second half. The move started when I won the ball just inside our own half and finished when Sylvain slotted in the rebound after Fabien Barthez had only pushed Ljungberg's shot into his path. Cue scenes of delirium among our travelling fans.

From that moment it was all about keeping our composure and seeing the game out in a professional manner, which we did. United were the defending champions and their players were very gracious in defeat and all shook our hands to congratulate us, but they quickly disappeared off the pitch. You expect that, because it was not their night, it was our night and we made sure we celebrated with the away fans who were lucky enough to get a ticket.

We flew back to London straight after the game and all went out on the town, which was pretty lively. Arsene, who used to enjoy a nice glass of wine himself, said we could do what we liked that night and simply told us to enjoy ourselves. It was a brilliant atmosphere among the lads and to win another Double was really exciting. At the end of your career it is not about how much money you have earned but how many medals you have managed to put in your cabinet.

I do not remember much about the celebrations but I know I did not get much sleep and would have stayed out for a couple of days afterwards. What a week that was. Fantastic.

PETER MARINELLO

Peter Marinello
Forward
1970–1973

The son of a barman of Italian descent and an Irish mother, Peter Marinello was born in Edinburgh on 20 February 1950 and grew up among the basic prefabs of Saughton housing estate where Graeme Souness was among his neighbours. A schoolboy winger of exceptional pace, Peter snubbed England legend Stanley Matthews, then in charge of Port Vale, and Chelsea manager Tommy Docherty, to turn professional in 1967 at local club Hibernian. Marinello, deemed talented enough by the British press to be dubbed 'the new George Best', made his high-profile £100,000 move south to Arsenal in January 1970 but featured in fewer than 40 league games for the Gunners, scoring three goals, before being transferred to Portsmouth in July 1973. His career drifting, Marinello made further ports of call at Motherwell, Canberra City, Fulham, Phoenix Inferno, Hearts, Partick Thistle and, finally, Broxburn Athletic. He made two appearances for Scotland Under-23s – but only three in the First Division during Arsenal's historic Double-winning campaign of 1970/71.

Manchester United 2-1 Arsenal

Division One
Saturday, 10 January 1970
Old Trafford, Manchester
Attendance: 41,055

Manchester United	Arsenal
Stepney	Wilson
Dunne (Sartori)	Nelson
Sadler	Neill
Ure	Simpson
Edwards	Storey
Burns	Armstrong
Aston	Court
Crerand	Sammels
Morgan	Marinello
Charlton	George
Kidd	Radford

Managers

Matt Busby	Bertie Mee

Goals

Sartori	Marinello
Morgan	

'Overwhelming' scarcely does justice to my hectic introduction to life in London at the end of the Swinging Sixties.

Arsenal were more than happy to pay the club's first six-figure fee to Hibs for my services, crying out for a crowd-pleaser to rival the appeal of a certain charismatic character at Manchester United.

I, too, was a young skinny winger with long, dark hair and a keen eye for fashion, a pin-up for the girls and, I suppose, a sprinkling of stardust with a talent to entertain and excite crowds. Inevitably, I was tagged 'the second George Best'. Years later, one writer cruelly remarked 'We never even got to see him become the first Peter Marinello' – but he was correct in some respects.

I thought I had the world at my feet but I squandered my talent, pissed most of it up against the wall. I'm the guy who wrote the manual, 'How Not To Do It'.

Yet in the very beginning at Arsenal, before I felt I had been swept up by a tornado and battered from pillar to post, life was sweet even if I was dubious about the overkill accompanying my signing under Bertie Mee's watchful gaze. For the benefit of a battery of Fleet Street photographers I stepped out that Friday on to the pitch in front of the North Bank wearing a fetching cream French-style mac I'd bought from the Jaeger store in Princes Street back home in Edinburgh. Within weeks, I'd started a trend and scores of young men about town were wearing a coat just like mine.

The signing was reported on the BBC television nine o'clock news and one Arsenal director claimed: 'We've signed the nearest thing in football to the Beatles.' No pressure, then.

My registration went through far too late for me to be eligible for the following day's FA Cup tie at home to Blackpool.

I was still only 19 and Bertie insisted he had bought me with the future in mind, and that I'd have to fight to get in the team, but I suppose the pressure the manager was under having sanctioned the huge £100,000 transfer fee and the fact George Graham travelled north carrying a slight injury, made my debut at Manchester United on 10 January a comfortable decision.

I didn't know for sure I was starting until we were in the away dressing room at Old Trafford, so there was no way I could arrange tickets for a coachload of Marinellos and Murrays, on mum's side of the family, to travel down from Scotland.

Unfortunately for the headline writers, George Best was also absent, fined £100 by the FA and starting a 28-day suspension for knocking the ball out of referee Jack Taylor's hands at the end of a League Cup semi-final against Manchester City.

Mind you, the press had a field day when Bestie came back to score six times in an 8-2 FA Cup win at Northampton. That was the absolute measure of a man who was undoubtedly a genius. No way on earth, or in my wildest dreams, was I equipped to score a double hat-trick.

But score I certainly did that day in Manchester after 14 minutes in a dream start. Terry Neill whacked the ball on from the centre circle, John Radford slipped through a teasing pass with potential, there was a lucky bounce but I was first to react. A bit of clever footwork left Ian Ure and Tony Dunne in my wake as I manipulated the ball right, left, then right again. Out came their goalkeeper Alex Stepney and I beat him with my shot low inside the far post. Job done, fist raised in a cheeky salute to the Stretford End, a 41,000 crowd silenced.

The instant the ball hit the net it seemed like the best thing in the world but that goal became a millstone. After that, I was expected to score every time I pulled on a pair of boots and the expectation weighed me down.

Maybe I should have had an inkling of what was coming down the line. The headline writers with 'Peter the Great' up their sleeves must have been as disappointed as me when another youngster of Italian heritage, Carlo Sartori, equalised for United and another Scot, Willie Morgan, upstaged me with the winner.

Back in London, it was a case of excess all areas. I married my glamorous girlfriend, Joyce, who joined the Lucie Clayton modelling agency, while I lived the high life, burning the candle at both ends and in the middle. The capital was like a big new toy and I was out most nights living the life of a playboy.

I've always liked a drink, no preference, just as long as it's wet, and there was an industrial quantity of booze on tap, gambling, celebrity parties, newspaper columns, advertising deals with Freemans mail order clothing catalogue, modelling for Nino Cerruti, an appearance on *Top of the Pops* with Tony Blackburn, drinks with Princess Margaret and Adam Faith, judging the Miss Great Britain contest.

I'd train in the morning then hit Soho and the West End – shows, meals, nightclubs, mini-skirted girls. That *Top of the Pops* show with Pan's People and my heart-throb Sandie Shaw, who was extremely shy, was a special memory, especially some of the sexual goings-on at the party afterwards.

Fellow Scot Lulu was quite a regular at Highbury and modelled with me for Freemans. George Best's agent Ken Stanley wanted me to open a string of boutiques with his client. I shudder to think of the collateral damage we would have caused.

George himself warned me after my debut: 'Peter, you've become public property and everyone will think they have the right to abuse you and take you to task on almost any issue. There will be so many thousands of letters, you'll need to employ a full-time staff to deal with them. Remember you need a person to sift through the filthy letters with all their obscenities before the young girls dealing with your mail are offended by them. I'm still learning to live with all this. Good luck, mate.'

Bestie was spot on about the abusive mail but wrong about needing a censor. Joyce willingly opened all my letters, sometimes as many as 400 a week, 80 per cent of them from teenage girls. She told me sniffily: 'Some of them are such drivel', but when I asked to have a look, she glared at me menacingly.

Another of my endorsements was with the Milk Marketing Board. Outside the Gunners pub at Highbury appeared this massive poster of me on a billboard, proclaiming: Drinka Pinta Milka Day... only some wag climbed up with a tin of black paint and turned the pint of milk in my hand into a pint of Guinness. All the lads lapped it up, but it didn't go down too well with Bertie Mee – although that reference to the stout wasn't far off the mark.

London was like the Promised Land, only it became ridiculous with offers to cut a pop record, become a film star and also an author. Everyone wanted a piece of me and I was easy meat.

Cameos rather than consistency were a feature of my Arsenal career but the supporters loved me, well most of them, especially the girls. I got the full treatment from the choirs of the North Bank and Clock End. Steam's No.1 chart hit 'Na Na Hey Hey Kiss Him Goodbye' was adapted to proclaim 'Marinello, Marinello, Hey Hey Marinello' and The Sandpipers' 'Guantanamera' became 'One Marinello, there's only one Marinello' while a line from Donovan's *Mellow Yellow* floated on the air as 'they call him Marinello'. It was complete madness becoming a cult figure without seriously achieving anything of note as a footballer for the club.

And I admit I never did myself many favours on the pitch, either. At Hibs, everything had come so naturally, it was a joy to play off the cuff and the pace I had developed working under a top-class sprinting coach made me difficult to catch in Scottish football.

Don Howe found me difficult to coach. Arsenal had a very structured, regimented way of playing and it wasn't designed to accommodate a maverick. I had never properly taken tactics on board and was still like an enthusiastic kid in the schoolyard wanting to be involved all the time, coming in off the wing to get a touch of the ball when the team needed to know where to find me, waiting out wide with chalk on my boots.

The other thing I did, unwittingly, which did me no favours was to put years and years on Geordie Armstrong's career at the club. I had been bought to replace him and the ever-popular Geordie was lined up to go to Newcastle United under Joe Harvey for a cut-price £15,000.

Arsenal never got anywhere near value for money from me, but they must have counted their blessings they never cashed in by selling Geordie.

The club have had some fabulous players – Dennis Bergkamp and Liam Brady spring readily to mind. But Geordie was as influential as them, believe me. He could clear the ball off our line one moment, beat two or three opponents in midfield in the tackle, bomb down the wing and cross, more accurately than me, for Raddy or 'Razor', Ray Kennedy, to head in.

Me? I was lazy and slack at first when it came to doing the dirty work and tracking back. I was all style, Geordie was all substance.

One time Don Howe was delivering a serious message and turned round to find me strumming an air guitar. My punishment was a gruelling afternoon on the training ground, and it was fully justified.

But what did I care? I was as much a playboy as a professional footballer.

There were some dodgy characters and gangsters attaching themselves to the team. I never met the Krays but one time Bob McNab had the Richardson brothers in the players' lounge until Bertie marked his card.

I was at a party in Finchley with a few of the other lads and a heavy mob. I told this bruiser I was having problems getting in the side because of Geordie's form, and he asked: 'Do you want me to shoot this Armstrong geezer, then?' I must have looked alarmed because he swiftly added: 'Nothing serious, just a leg job.' I made my apologies and left, flagging down a taxi and looking anxiously over my shoulder.

I did have my moments as an Arsenal player, though, but they aren't happy memories. I started against Ajax in the 3-0 first leg win of the 3-0 Inter-Cities Fairs Cup semi-final win in April 1970, only for Geordie to come on to replace me and stay in the team for the final victory against Anderlecht. That brought Arsenal their first trophy since 1953.

I had a golden chance in March 1972 in the European Cup. We were 2-1 down from the first leg in the quarter-finals against Johan Cruyff's Ajax and, for once, Bertie Mee decided to go gung-ho with me, wearing the No.9 shirt, on one wing and Geordie on the other. The game was in its infancy when the Dutch cocked up completely trying to play out from defence; I easily robbed the full-back Wim Suurbier and glory beckoned. But from near the penalty spot my shot was too tame, not precise enough, the goalkeeper Heinz Stuy dropped on it and I turned away in bitter disappointment.

Every Arsenal function I attend, a fan of a certain age is guaranteed to remind me of that miss and say we would have won the European Cup that year had I scored.

It took me 14 minutes to be a hit at Arsenal, but that miss has haunted me all my life.

MALCOLM MACDONALD

Malcolm Macdonald
Striker
1976–1979

Malcolm Macdonald revelled in his 'Supermac' nickname. Born and raised near Fulham's ground, Macdonald was one of the most exciting and prolific goalscorers of his era during a career which took in Tonbridge, Fulham, Luton, Newcastle and Arsenal. By the time a knee injury had forced him into premature retirement at 29, Macdonald had amassed 260 senior goals in 488 appearances plus another six for England, including five in one game against Cyprus. For whoever he played, Macdonald was a cult hero. Blessed with blistering pace, a cannonball of a left foot and exceptional ability in the air for someone not six feet tall, Macdonald rejected interest from Spurs to join the Gunners for the curious fee of £333,333.34. In two hectic years he rattled in 57 goals in 108 appearances but statistics alone fail to do him justice. Twice he earned the Golden Boot, once at Newcastle and once at Arsenal. In his first season he scored 29 goals for the Gunners and in his second, 26 in 52. But the injury, sustained in a League Cup tie at Rotherham, stopped him adding to his considerable tally and deprived Arsenal fans of a talisman. Macdonald was equally revered on Tyneside and was looking forward to facing his old club for the first time ... until Newcastle manager Gordon Lee made some ill-judged comments.

Arsenal 5-3 Newcastle United

Division One
Saturday, 4 December 1976
Highbury, London
Attendance: 35,000

Arsenal	Newcastle
Rimmer	Mahoney
Rice (Matthews)	Nattrass
Nelson	McCaffrey
O'Leary	Kennedy
Howard	Cassidy
Armstrong	Craig
Ball	Nulty
Brady	Gowling
Ross	Burns
Macdonald	Cannell
Stapleton	Barrowclough

Managers

Terry Neill	Gordon Lee

Goals

Macdonald (3)	Burns (2)
Stapleton	Gowling
Ross	

Newcastle was a club close to my heart – and still are – but when Gordon Lee replaced Joe Harvey as manager I knew my time was up. Lee got rid of Terry Hibbitt, a high-class midfield player, and we had a conversation soon afterwards which made it very clear I was not part of his plans. Only he knows why, because I had scored a century of goals for them and the fans loved me. Maybe that was the trouble. Anyway, Arsenal came in for me and I couldn't have joined a better club. I might only have been there a couple of years but had a fabulous time. The place ran like clockwork, everything was brilliantly organised and from top to bottom it was a well-oiled machine. I loved my time at Arsenal and was just beginning to reach my prime when I was injured. Such a shame. I felt I had so much more to give.

Anyway, when Newcastle came down to Highbury in early December, the country was paralysed by snow and ice and our game only went ahead because our pitch had undersoil heating. Even so there were parts of it that day that were icy and difficult, but at least we played. BBC's *Match of the Day* had a big slot to fill and only the one game on, so they must have been happy with eight goals and plenty of incident.

There was much more to this match than the goals, because the background was decidedly unpleasant. I had expected to be a little emotional playing against my old club and their tremendous fans. Instead, I was filled with anger and determination and for that I can thank Gordon Lee.

One day in training a few days before the game, Alan Ball, a great player and a good friend, came into the dressing room brandishing a newspaper, possibly *The Sun*. 'Have you see this?' he said to me. I had not. On examination, there was a big article attributed to Gordon Lee, slagging me off in an unbelievable fashion. He accused me of being a glory-hunter and a headline-seeker. It was extraordinary stuff from an opposition manager and needlessly nasty. In fact, I'd had a conversation with Lee along these lines before I joined Arsenal, so it was not completely new. My response then was that I scored goals for a living; it was my job and anyone who scored goals inevitably made the headlines. But here he was, saying the same things in a high-circulation newspaper. I was quite shocked, if only because, although I knew he didn't like me, I never expected him to say so in print. Bally was even more furious than I was and pinned the offending story on the dressing-room wall. 'Every one of you should read this,' Ball told the rest of the team before the kick-off. 'Our job is to make sure Malcolm gets all the goals and rams Lee's words down his throat.'

So there was a real edge to this match, none of it apparent to a television audience, of course, but the whole team was fired up on my behalf. To this day, I don't know why Lee said those words. He couldn't say he had been taken out of context or that he had spoken off the record. This was what he thought about me and he was obviously keen to make it public.

Micky Burns, a lovely lad, put Newcastle ahead before Trevor Ross, one of many fine young players coming through the Arsenal system, equalised. Then I put us ahead and Frank Stapleton made the best of my flick-on to make it 3-1. I got another and then hit the bar and had a couple of good shots well saved by Mick Mahoney. I could have got a hat-trick by half-time. Newcastle replied through Alan Gowling and Burns before I had the huge satisfaction of getting my third. In the circumstances, it was very sweet.

One of my goals was a pure piece of class from Ball. I had told him how Alan Kennedy had a tendency to run under a long ball played to his side of the pitch and Bally placed it perfectly for me to score with a header. Thank you very much, Alan. Another of my goals came as a result of a mishit shot by Stapleton which found me unmarked at the far post. I remember Frank saying: 'How did he know I was going to mishit it?' In truth, we were better than 5-3; Ball and Liam Brady were exhilarating in midfield and set up numerous openings.

This was my way of shutting up Gordon Lee. I looked at him suffering in the dugout but there was no response, no hint of recognition. I didn't find him after the match and I don't think I even went looking for him. What would have been the point? My goals had done my talking for me. In fact, I didn't see him for many years, not until I was manager of Fulham and he was in charge of Leicester's youth team. He looked at me sheepishly but no words were spoken. Winding me up was acceptable, part of the game, but what he said in that newspaper article was a character assassination and all it did was anger our entire dressing room. I had never seen Alan Ball so livid.

I may have finished my playing career five or six years early but I look back on it with great fondness, not least my years in an Arsenal shirt. Talking of which, and this is typical of the whole club, I love the way they look after their ex-players. I was invited down to a match in the last days of Highbury when I was to be honoured with others who had scored hat-tricks for the club. But when I woke up on the day of the match, the snow was about 12 feet deep outside my front door, the roads were blocked and the trains struggling to keep going. I had to cry off.

Anyway, I was invited down again for the last match at the old stadium, against Wigan. The Emirates was almost ready and this was going to be a nostalgic day for all of us who loved the old place. I actually parked my car at the Emirates on my way to Highbury and, as I did so, a girl in an Arsenal uniform came up and said: 'I've got something for you.'

She took me over to a spot where she suddenly produced a package. 'This is for you,' she said. 'You were not able to come down for the hat-trick scorers' day earlier in the season when the weather was bad but we have kept this for you.'

Inside was a replica of an Arsenal shirt from the very first days of the club's existence, a reddy purple with the number nine on the back. I was amazed they had had time to think about something so trivial when there was a big move only days away, but they had. Arsenal were like that. They still remembered what I had done in my short spell all those years before and it was a wonderful gesture. It was a classy thing to do and I shall treasure it forever.

All of which was a very far cry from my humble origins in the game. Scoring hat-tricks for Arsenal was the last thing on my mind, growing up close to Craven Cottage. As an eight-year-old I was given an autograph book and I used to wait near the bus stop for the Fulham players to get off and make their way to the stadium. One day, a young Bobby Robson, then an aspiring wing-half, was spotted and was much needed for my book. I walked up alongside him and politely asked if he would sign it for me. Robson handed me his kit bag, exchanged it for my pen and book, and walked on. That kit bag was heavy.

Eventually he asked me if I played football and I told him I did. I told him that I would like to be a footballer when I grew up. 'What position?' he replied. Struggling to keep going with Bobby's bag, I told him I played in any position I was needed. 'You must be one of the better players,' he said. Then he asked with what foot I kicked. 'Left,' I said, and his eyes lit up.

'You will always get a game in that case,' said Bobby. 'There is always a place in a team for a natural left-footer. They widen the pitch. Playing a right-footed player on the left is never the same. They cut inside.' With that, he signed my book and disappeared into the stadium.

Ten years later I was playing non-league football for Tonbridge, often as a full-back. I was told Fulham were interested in me, as were Crystal Palace. I asked if I could speak to Fulham, by now managed by Robson. They agreed and off I went to Craven Cottage, a stadium I knew well. The girl at reception pointed to Robson's office door down the corridor.

I knocked on the door and entered. Robson was deeply engrossed in a letter and neither looked up at me standing the other side of his desk or even acknowledged my existence. For five minutes I stood there uncomfortably as Robson read the letter. It seemed like an eternity. Eventually he put it down and stared ... and stared, squinting as he examined me.

Suddenly he said: 'I know you. You were the little squirt at the bus stop who followed me to the ground, pleading for an autograph. You wouldn't shut up.' I was later told by Eric Gates, who played for Robson at Ipswich, that it was a tactic of Robson's to pretend he was busy to make players such as myself, seeking a contract, feel uneasy.

This time it was my turn to do the signing. I joined Fulham there and then, moved on to Luton and then to Newcastle where I thoroughly enjoyed my time until Gordon Lee came along.

Had he not made it clear I was not wanted at Newcastle, I might never have found my way to Arsenal. So, in a way, I have to thank him for two wonderful years.

We had some great players coming through, which was one of the reasons I signed for the Gunners: Brady, Stapleton, O'Leary, Rix, Devine, Price and others. I could see them going from strength to strength. Alan Ball was a fabulous player and was another reason I chose Arsenal over Tottenham. There were also people like George Armstrong, who has got to be the fittest footballer I ever knew. He ran and ran and ran. During pre-season, when the rest of us were gasping in the breaks between running and exercises, Geordie would play a game of tennis and then again after we had all finished. He was a great enthusiast and should have played for England.

DAVID O'LEARY

David O'Leary
Defender
1975–1993

No player has made more than David O'Leary's 722 league and cup appearances for Arsenal spread over almost two decades of outstanding club and personal success. His record is unlikely ever to be beaten. London-born but raised in Dublin, O'Leary was among a group of world-class players to find their way to Arsenal from Ireland, north and south. Pat Jennings, Pat Rice, John Devine, Sammy Nelson, Liam Brady, Frank Stapleton and O'Leary were mainstays of an Arsenal side assembled gradually in the 70s and 80s who went on to dominate the domestic English scene. O'Leary made his debut at 18 in 1975 and hardly missed a match in the next decade, making his 400th club appearance when still only 28. A tall, cultured and pacy central defender, on his day there were few better players in his position in the league than O'Leary. It was a sad day for Gunners fans when he eventually headed north to Leeds for a brief career finale. He later managed Leeds, Aston Villa and Al-Ahli and is now back among the Arsenal family as a club ambassador. During his glittering 19 years at Highbury, O'Leary collected two league titles, twice won the FA Cup and twice the League Cup. Three times he was named in the PFA's Team of the Year between 1978 and 1982.

O'Leary featured in many outstanding matches in Arsenal's red and white but if there is one small blemish on his astonishing record it is that he never quite brought home European silverware. He got close in 1979/80 but, as he explains, not close enough.

Juventus 0-1 Arsenal

European Cup Winners' Cup semi-final, second leg
Wednesday, 23 April 1980
Stadio Comunale, Turin
Attendance: 66,386

Juventus	**Arsenal**
Zoff	Jennings
Cabrini	Devine
Cuccureddu	Rice
Gentile	O'Leary
Scirea	Young
Fanna	Brady
Furino	Price (Vaessen)
Prandelli (Marocchino)	Talbot (Hollins)
Tavola	Rix
Bettega	Stapleton
Causio	Sunderland

Managers

Giovanni Trapattoni — Terry Neill

Goal

Vaessen

The three great matches of my life were the 1979 FA Cup Final win over Manchester United, the incredible last-ditch victory at Liverpool to win the league in 1989 and the penalty I scored for the Republic of Ireland against Romania to take us through to the World Cup quarter-finals in 1990. There were many others I was fortunate to experience but few more thrilling than our win over a very strong Juventus side in a packed and raucous Stadio Comunale in 1980. To set the scene, the first leg was played at Highbury and we could only manage a 1-1 draw. So Juventus, on their own ground and in front of 66,000 fanatical supporters, were overwhelming favourites to finish the job. With an away goal to cushion them, all they had to do was stop us scoring in the second leg to book a place in the final against Valencia. That first leg was a tough affair and one I won't forget in a hurry because I still have a scar to show for it. Roberto Bettega was one of the best players in the world at the time and finished this particular season as Serie A's top scorer. As a striker he was quick and strong and had been Italy's main forward for some time. He was obviously going to be a handful for myself and my central defensive partner, Willie Young.

What I had not expected was to be carried off after 23 minutes, the victim of a very nasty tackle by Bettega, which should have been punished with a red card. My shin pad saved me from serious injury but, as I say, the war wounds from his high challenge remain 40 years later as a permanent reminder. By then we were already a goal down, Antonio Cabrini scoring from a rebound after Pat Jennings had saved his spot kick. Sadly, we had been the architects of this particular setback with some poor defensive work, leaving us with a huge amount to do if we were going to save the match and keep alive the tie.

Juventus had some wonderful players, but for the rest of the game – and for the entire second leg two weeks later – they simply sat on their lead and invited us forward. They weren't prepared to let us play, either. Marco Tardelli was sent off in the 38th minute and with ten men they clung on behind a packed defence until five minutes from the end when Bettega, under pressure from Frank Stapleton, turned the ball into his own net. So justice was done, but you could tell Juventus were more than happy with the result because they felt they had done the hard part in coming to London, getting a draw and with it that precious away goal. Renowned for their defensive qualities, the Italians clearly believed they could smother and stifle us into submission when we met them a second time.

Terry Neill and Don Howe simply reminded us how we needed to be positive when we went to Turin. On the one hand, we had to be defensively secure, and on the other, we had to get a goal. Nothing else would have done.

What we had not expected once the match got under way was Juventus's complete lack of attacking ambition. It was not as though we had to weather attack after attack, because this highly talented Juventus side, packed with experienced, high-quality internationals, just sat back and waited for us to have a go at them. It was extraordinary. With the players they had at their disposal and the crowd behind them, we thought they would have thrown away their caution and done some attacking, but they never did.

At half-time and with the second leg still goalless, Neill and Howe were happy with our progress. Defensively, we were untroubled, but we still needed somehow to breach that packed defence of theirs and snatch a goal. The Juventus crowd were celebrating throughout, convinced they had won already, and those celebrations grew in intensity throughout the second half as the minutes ticked away. Flags were flying, horns were sounding and the noise was deafening. You could hear cries of 'Olé' all around this huge, intimidating arena as we mounted one attack after another without ever looking like we might find a way through. Paul Vaessen and John Hollins came on to give us fresh legs and towards the end it looked like Arsenal were the home team, so dominant were we in terms of possession.

Then in the 88th minute, just as we were beginning to abandon hope, we pushed forward in one last desperate attack. The crowd were whistling, counting down the seconds, when Graham Rix wriggled down the left and crossed brilliantly for Vaessen to bundle the ball over the line. No one could have missed from that range and the goal owed everything to Rix's amazing cross under pressure.

Cue complete silence. Where once the terraces were alive with happiness and bouncing with premature joy, now there was nothing, save for a few Arsenal fans in the corner suddenly rejuvenated and full of joy. The Juventus flags disappeared, 66,000 fans were hushed and headed for the exits. The transformation was incredible.

The Juventus players were similarly shell-shocked. They were on their knees, devastated by the extraordinary twist. There was still a minute or two left to be played but there was no late rally, no rush to abandon defence and test our nerve. Looking at our shell-shocked opponents, you could see in their eyes they had had enough. Their strategy, based around one of the best defences in world football, had failed them at the last. Within seconds it was all over and, while our own celebrations began, Juventus made their way off the pitch, crushed by our audacity.

We had a drink or two on the coach as we filed through the Turin streets and more back at the hotel, where we reflected on what we had achieved. It was a superb result by any standards and no more than we deserved for our determination not to give up.

I have to say this was a very good Arsenal side. Juventus were strong, but so were we. We had in Jennings one of the best goalkeepers in the world. In fact, that night in Turin, I think the two best keepers were on show in Jennings and Dino Zoff. They were similar in that they had a calmness about them which so helped defenders. They ruled their box with great efficiency and the minimum of fuss.

But the hero of the hour was undoubtedly Paul Vaessen, the young striker who came on late and got the winner even later. In many ways it is his memorial, because he died tragically young aged just 39 and in such unfortunate circumstances after his life had taken a sinister turn to drugs abuse and petty crime. Here in Turin, he carved himself a piece of Arsenal history. Paul was a nice, friendly lad, happy-go-lucky and not short of ability. He was never going to be another Stapleton, who was a great player, but he gave everything when he had his limited chances.

All around the pitch we had quality players, none more so than Liam Brady who, on the back of a fine display over two legs, got himself a move to Juventus where he flourished. Liam was a wizard on the ball, creating magic and making things happen. He would be the first to agree that his skills were complemented by the hard graft of the tireless Brian Talbot and the unsung David Price. Price was a bread-and-butter player but incredibly consistent and occasionally overlooked for his contributions week in and week out. The two full-backs, Pat Rice and Sammy Nelson, were as good as anyone in the English league and big Willie Young was a solid and strong defender alongside me. Again, we complemented each other. John Devine, who played in this particular match, came over from Dublin at much the same time as me and was hampered by injuries throughout his career so that we did not always see the best of his talent.

I can't forget Graham Rix either. What a good player he was on that left wing. Time and again he made goals for us with his skill and trickery. I take nothing away from Paul Vaessen's glory, but Rix was so instrumental in his goal's creation.

Up front we had Stapleton and Alan Sunderland; again, a pair who worked well together and brought different strengths. Alan scored some vital goals for us but by now Stapleton, another Dubliner, had become the complete centre-forward. What a great player he was. It was a bad moment for us when he chose to leave for Manchester United, our greatest rivals at the time. We tried to keep him, of course; the last thing we wanted was for him to go off and play for another English side, particularly United.

Anyway, the defeat of Juventus put us into the final at the Heysel Stadium against another strong team in Valencia. They had top players like Rainer Bonhof and Mario Kempes and it was another tough old clash between two sides not prepared to give an inch. The match ended 0-0 and went to penalties, where we lost 5-4. It was a disappointment because there was nothing between the sides, not many chances and it was hard physically. Brady missed our first penalty and Rix the last, so all our efforts over two legs against Juventus came to nothing eventually. The players we thought would score from the spot did not and those we might have doubted (Stapleton, Sunderland, Talbot and Hollins) did. That's football.

That was as close as I got to winning in Europe with Arsenal. It would have been nice to have had something to show for our efforts beyond the English league, but you can't have everything. I had a wonderful time over many happy years with Arsenal and picked up plenty of trophies and accolades, so I would never complain or have regrets. I was a lucky man.

PERRY GROVES

Perry Groves
Midfielder
1986–1992

Perry Groves was the only true Cockney in the Arsenal side that won the League Cup, then sponsored by Littlewoods, in 1986/87. Born within the sound of Bow Bells at St Barts on 19 April 1965, but raised in Essex, Groves fulfilled a lifetime's ambition when he joined the club he supported as a boy, from Fourth Division Colchester for £75,000 in September 1986, aged 21. All his family were Gooners and his uncle, Vic Groves, had played with distinction for Arsenal as a wing-half from 1955 to 1964. Perry Groves spent six years with the club he adored until 1992 when he was transferred to Southampton for £750,000. Sadly, the move did not work out, a serious Achilles tendon injury restricting him to only 15 appearances for Saints (and two goals) before he was forced into premature retirement at 29. For his beloved Gunners, the pacy winger played 155 times and scored 21 goals without ever being sure of a regular first-team place because of the intense competition. He had the distinction of being George Graham's first signing and went on to become a cult figure among Arsenal fans, who loved him for his energy, skill and commitment. They sang 'We all live in a Perry Groves world' to the tune of The Beatles' 'Yellow Submarine' and later that chant became the title of Groves's autobiography, which went on to become a best-seller, outstripping the book brought out at the same time by the less popular (among Arsenal fans) Ashley Cole. Groves went from Colchester's homely Layer Road to Wembley in the space of just a few months.

Arsenal 2-1 Liverpool

League Cup Final
Sunday, 5 April 1987
Wembley, London
Attendance: 96,000

Arsenal	Liverpool
Lukic	Grobbelaar
Anderson	Gillespie
O'Leary	Venison
Adams	Spackman
Sansom	Whelan
Rocastle	Hansen
Davis	Walsh (Dalglish)
Williams	Johnston
Hayes (Thomas)	Rush
Quinn (Groves)	Molby
Nicholas	McMahon (Wark)

Managers
George Graham   Kenny Dalglish

Goals
Nicholas (2)   Rush

I was lucky even to be playing in this match because I could so easily have been cup-tied. Colchester played Peterborough in the first round and, as a regular in the Colchester team, I would have played but for a curious twist of fate. My nan died so I was given a bit of compassionate leave and missed the game. How sick would I have felt, seven short months later, if I had been forced to sit in the Wembley stands as a spectator. I got lucky, I guess. Even though I was a newcomer from a lower division background, George Graham had me in and around the first team and I played my part in getting us to Wembley. We needed three matches to get past our deadly rivals Tottenham in the semi-final, losing the first leg 1-0, a match in which I got injured, and winning the second leg 2-1 before scraping home in a replay.

When it came to the final, I thought my close friend Ian Allinson was more likely to play than me. Ian and I shared digs at Colchester, where we were players together, and then I followed him to Arsenal. We knew Ian as 'Blimpy' and when I joined Arsenal I stayed at his house. We got on extremely well together and since he had scored in one of those Spurs matches I was pretty certain he would get one of the two substitutes' shirts. This was at a time when teams were only allowed two subs and the manager decided he would have a defender or midfield player for one of them and a forward for the other. Michael Thomas, a rapidly developing young talent, got the first role and the other was between me and Blimpy. On the eve of the match after a good week's training, George told me that I was going to be the other sub. Naturally I was elated and excited at the prospect of playing at a packed-out Wembley, yet I couldn't help but be disappointed for my pal Ian. But he wished me all the best as a team-mate and gentleman, as I like to think I would have done if it had been the other way around.

George named his line-up on the Saturday morning. It is in moments like that when he is going through the names that you have to pinch yourself that it is actually happening. I could so easily have joined Millwall or Steve Coppell's Crystal Palace, but instead fate pointed me towards Arsenal and here I was taking part in a Wembley final.

Everything pointed to a Liverpool win. Kenny Dalglish, their player-manager, had assembled an incredible team without any weaknesses and packed with experienced, high-class internationals in every position. They had won the League and FA Cup Double in 1986, while it's fair to say George Graham's Arsenal were still very much a work in progress. His team – our team – was short of Liverpool's class and consistency and our league form, if that was any true guide, was no match for Liverpool's. Arsenal were in their centenary year and it was eight long years since we had last appeared in a final. Not only would it have been nice to celebrate a club landmark with a win but also there was the incentive of the winners being able to take part in European competition the following season.

Some 50 Colchester fans in a coachload were coming up to see the match and they made it clear they wanted to see me in action at some stage. I was going around among the other Arsenal players begging and borrowing tickets to make sure they all got in among this colossal crowd which thronged the streets and byways leading to the Twin Towers. The last thing I wanted was to remain on the bench and not get a chance to show them I belonged at this level.

Was I nervous? Very much so, but in an excited sort of way. So too were the more experienced players, who told me that butterflies were good for you because it got the adrenalin going and gave your performance an edge. I remember also they told me to soak up all the sights and sounds of the big occasion because it might never happen to me again. Wise advice, and as a result I do recall a surprising amount of what happened that wonderful day.

We had not won for nine or ten matches so we were hardly bang in form, while the Liverpool machine showed no signs of creaking, so it was hardly a surprise that we were the underdogs and George Graham was aware of this. That is why his pre-match team talk was so special. It was one of the best I ever heard. One by one, player by player, George went through the Liverpool team and instead of acknowledging their strengths, which would have been easy to do, concentrated on what he perceived to be their faults. For instance, he said the goalkeeper Bruce Grobbelaar often came for crosses he was never going to get and said the central defensive pairing of Alan Hansen and Gary Gillespie was no longer the quickest. As he demolished them individually, you could see our morale being lifted. We were not playing supermen. The one exception to his criticisms was Ian Rush, because George loved Rush. He knew, as we all did, that Rush could destroy teams with his brilliant running and deadly finishing, but he did question his attitude. Would he be up for such an occasion? The Littlewoods Cup Final was not going to be Liverpool's biggest match of the season, even if it was ours. It was brilliant psychology by our manager, who used his flip chart to pinpoint a fault in every one of those great players. I'm sure his inspirational team talk had so much to do with our success that memorable day.

As we went on to the famous Wembley turf that afternoon to the roars of both sets of fans (plus 50 from Colchester) I couldn't help but look at our left-back Kenny Sansom and think to myself how the previous June I had been watching him play for England against Argentina in the World Cup and thinking what a great player he was. Now I was playing alongside him.

Liverpool had never lost a match in which the prolific Rush had scored, something like 144, so the omens were not good for us when he scored in the 23rd minute. I suppose, on the run of play, it was deserved, if I'm being fair. George had got us well drilled, our shape was good and within seven minutes we were level. Viv Anderson crossed from the right and Charlie Nicholas scored with a goal which went in off a post. After coasting for half an hour, you could see that our equaliser had knocked a little wind from Liverpool's sails and the rest of the first half was evenly contested. It's an odd feeling being a sub. You are an interested spectator like the other 96,000 in the stadium but at any moment you know you can be hauled from your anonymous seat to take part in it. Every now and then I ran up and down the touchline to remind the manager I was available. At the break I found out I would be needed. George was convinced Liverpool would tire. They were not a young side and sometimes the sheer weight of a big occasion can sap the legs and drain the energy of even the most capable of players. George said to me to be mentally ready. The last thing players like Hansen and Gillespie wanted in the last 20 minutes or so was to see someone like me, full of youthful zest, come on and buzz around in front of them. And that's precisely what happened.

With about 20 minutes plus added time left George sent me on, wearing number 12, in place of Niall Quinn who had been a strong physical presence all afternoon. Dalglish brought himself on at much the same time and, while he was past his prime, he was always going to be influential. It was not going to be easy coming on quite late in the game. I had to remember who Quinn had been marking at corners and set pieces and yet do what the manager wanted me to do, namely run at a tiring defence. In a strange, inexplicable way I knew it was going to be my day from the moment of my first touch. A long clearance came from our goalkeeper and, as I backed into Gillespie, I controlled it perfectly and laid it off. After that, everything I did came off. I even crash-tackled the not inconsiderable figure of Jan Molby and came away the victor. This got the Arsenal fans on my side and I could feel my confidence grow.

My big match-winning moment came in the 83rd minute. Sansom hoofed the ball, and I use that word deliberately, down the left wing and I like to think I made his clearance into a good pass when I collected it near the touchline. The left side was not my best and I could feel Gillespie, who as George predicted was visibly tiring, coming in to tackle. He slid in and was gone, I knew not where, and as I got a touch away from him, I was free. Suddenly Liverpool were exposed. I cut inside towards the Liverpool goal and was left with a choice. If I had been on my stronger right side I would have had a shot but I was going to have to do whatever I did with my weaker foot. I slowed down as I got into the box, wondering what to do next, and spotted Nicholas out of the corner of my eye moving into a better position. I passed it to him 15 yards out and he hit it first time. Luckily my pass had had just enough pace on it and Charlie's shot, deflected by Ronnie Whelan, managed to wrong-foot Grobbelaar who didn't move as the ball went into the net. All the great sportsmen will tell you how their finest moments always seemed to happen in slow motion and, while I would never put myself in that bracket, this shot seemed to take about 20 seconds to go into the net. I remember saying to myself: 'Oh my god, it's gone in.' It was an incredible feeling, absolutely sensational, something that brings the goosebumps every time I recall it.

What it did was rouse Liverpool. They had fewer than ten minutes to save the game and with people like Dalglish on the pitch that was still enough time to salvage an equaliser and even a winner. It was the longest ten minutes of our lives. In Steve Williams we had the right player to see out time. Steve was the perfect game-manager and we survived with not as many scares as we feared. At the final whistle there was bedlam of course. Liverpool congratulated us although their disappointment was clear and, as George Graham had rightly foretold, they looked fatigued. Each of us went up and received a small replica of the cup itself and Sansom collected the real thing. Yet again my mind went back to how he was playing for England a year ago and I was a fan.

We did three laps of honour around the pitch and Arsenal were back in business, back in Europe and on the way to becoming a force once more. It was George's first season as manager and it was the beginning of a bright new era for the club. From a personal perspective, I was just happy that my dad, Arnold, another ginger and a long-distance lorry driver, was there to witness my finest hour. Dad was my biggest fan and biggest critic. He drove me around the country when I was a kid and missed only about four of my games up to the age of 18. I owed him a huge amount for believing in me when others appeared not to. I was rejected as a boy by Wolves and then by Peterborough. When Peter Morris, the boss at Peterborough, said there was no place for me after trials, Dad grabbed him by the throat. I was also turned down by Norwich, Ipswich, Southend and Luton before Colchester offered me an apprenticeship. This win was his reward as well as mine.

What of our team that day? John Lukic was underestimated and, at the time, one of the best four goalkeepers in the country. He was reliable, honest and would earn a mark of eight out of ten every week. George had nothing against him at all but, when the chance came to sign David Seaman, he knew he was bringing in the best. Viv Anderson was the worst trainer I ever saw but George let him get away with it because Viv delivered when it mattered on match days. David O'Leary served Arsenal for 700 matches and he had that long stride which made him deceptively quick. Alongside him was the young Tony Adams, 'Rodders' as we called him, because he resembled Rodney from *Only Fools and Horses*. He was learning his trade in 1987 and relied on O'Leary at times but we could see a captain-in-waiting even then. I suggest Sansom was the best left-back the club ever had. His shorts never got dirty and there was a reason for that: he never needed to dive in because he had such great balance.

The mere mention of David Rocastle makes me smile and makes me sad. He was dead at 33 but if anyone doubts his quality I refer them to YouTube and a match against Manchester United when he beats Paul Ince and Bryan Robson and chips Peter Schmeichel from 30 yards. Rocky could tackle, take people on, run with the ball and, on top of that, he was handsome and humble. The only problem was that he played in my position. Paul Davis was the perfect foil for Steve Williams in the centre of midfield. He looked like a twig because he was so thin, and off the pitch was a quiet man. Williams was a top-class player with everything at his disposal and in Martin Hayes we had a left-winger who had brilliant feet and was a cool finisher. One season he got 24 goals for us and was unlucky in that, after being sold to Celtic, he broke his leg.

Quinn was much the same age as me and we came into the team at the same time. He was 6ft 4in and was known as 'baby giraffe'. I loved playing alongside him and he had that ability to make others like me look good. He was still learning in 1987 like me, Hayes and Adams and I felt sorry for him when George went out and bought Alan Smith, forcing him to move away to get games. Charlie Nicholas, the two-goal hero, was one of the most technically gifted players of his generation, great with his back to goal and backing into defenders. Arsenal fans loved him because he chose to join us over Liverpool from Celtic and on his day he was capable of great brilliance. Charlie's two goals that day earned him a new two-year contract on improved terms. He never thanked me. Lastly, there was Michael Thomas, the strongest man in the team, a player with a brilliant engine and tremendous stamina, another player of high calibre in the making. The spirit among us was tremendous.

Over the next few years I was part of the squad that won the league title in 1988/89 and 1990/91 and which went back to Wembley in 1988 as hot favourites to retain the League Cup against Luton. I really don't want to talk about that one.

PAUL DAVIS

Paul Davis
Midfielder
1980–1995

Dulwich-born Paul Davis was the original member of Arsenal's fabled south London talent factory, which later saw Michael Thomas and David Rocastle rise to title-winning prominence. A boyhood Gunners fan, Davis came up through the youth ranks before spending 15 years in the first team and accumulating 447 appearances and 37 goals. The cultured midfielder, regarded as one of the best Arsenal players never to turn out for England, was part of the victorious league championship sides of 1989 and 1991 and won four other major trophies before brief spells in Norway and at Brentford following his departure from Highbury in 1995. Davis spent seven years on the Arsenal backroom staff between 1996 and 2003 and later joined the FA as a coach. Having battled racial prejudice during his playing days, Davis also became an ambassador for 'Kick it Out' and 'Show Racism the Red Card'. Davis made his Arsenal debut as a 17-year-old in a north London derby remembered for being 'the day Arsenal's reserves beat Tottenham's first team'.

Tottenham 1-2 Arsenal

Division One
Monday, 7 April 1980
White Hart Lane, London
Attendance: 41,365

Tottenham	Arsenal
Daines	Barron
Hughton	Rice
Miller	O'Leary
Perryman	Young
McAllister	Walford
Ardiles	Brady (Sunderland)
Pratt	Davis
Galvin	Devine
Hoddle	Hollins
Yorath	Talbot
Jones	Vaessen

Managers

Keith Burkinshaw	Terry Neill

Goals

Jones	Vaessen
	Sunderland

Arsenal fans were left in a state of despair when Liam Brady was sold to Juventus in the summer of 1980 after tormenting his new employers in the Inter-Cities Fairs Cup, but I was not crying, even though as one of English football's finest he had been my role model and inspiration.

As a young kid making my way in the game Liam was the one player that I really admired and tried to emulate for his footballing ability and the way he played. I tried to model some of my game on his and there is no doubting that he was fabulous to watch, a true Highbury hero.

But he also played in my position, so the fact he upped sticks to Turin was the catalyst for me to play on a more regular basis. If he had not left, I do not know where my career would have gone, because there was no way I could have taken his place from him. I guess you can say Liam played a huge part in my development in more ways than one!

I actually made my debut alongside Liam, a day I will never forget. I was only 17 when I got the tap on the shoulder from manager Terry Neill to tell me I would be starting the north London derby at White Hart Lane and that my job would be to stifle the great Glenn Hoddle. No pressure, then.

People often ask me who was the toughest opponent I played against and I always say, without question, it was Glenn. I never faced another player like him and he had such a high skill level.

He is a few years older than me and was already well established and making a big name for himself by the time we first came toe-to-toe. That was something I was very conscious of, facing a player of his renowned ability.

Before the game, I was instructed that Glenn was someone we should mark closely and a big part of my role was to nullify his game and to stop him getting into any space because we all knew he was someone who could really hurt us. We all respected him and he was something else as a player, but that day we did manage to restrict him.

I played against Glenn many times in my career and he was the opponent I feared more than anybody else. I came up against Bryan Robson and Graeme Souness, two more greats, but nobody was as formidable as him.

Whenever I played against Glenn or, further down the line, Paul Gascoigne, I always had to be aware they could do something special at any given moment so you could never relax or feel you had their measure and that mindset definitely helped me.

Glenn's biggest attribute was that he was equally good on both feet, a rare commodity even now and virtually unheard of in those days. If a player was right footed you were taught to show them on to their left foot or vice versa, but because he could go either side he had this little shimmy that he used to do to trick his marker into going one way, and then would check back and go the other. In that split second, he would be away.

He was also so gifted that he could almost do what he wanted with the ball if you gave him the space. For example, most of us could see a 40-yard pass into a striker but did not have the ability to deliver it at the right moment, but Glenn could do that nine times out of ten.

I feel for Glenn because I think he should have easily won 100 England caps, but he played at a time when that type of player was not really recognised. One of the reasons I admired him so much was because I wanted to be that type of player – to be creative, find passes and entertain the crowd – but those attributes were not as celebrated back then.

It is every player's dream to turn out for their country and it is frustrating that I am not able to say I did that. I got close and was selected for Graham Taylor's squad and also one of Bobby Robson's, but never managed to get on the pitch and pull on a Three Lions jersey. It is my one big regret.

Back to that Bank Holiday Monday in April 1980 and Terry brought in half a dozen youngsters because we were in the semi-finals of the Fairs Cup and the FA Cup, so he wanted to rest the senior players as we had nothing to play for in the league.

Paul Vaessen, who was the same age as me, played and scored our first goal, but Terry left out key players including Graham Rix so we definitely had an under-strength team, whereas Tottenham fielded a full side with Ossie Ardiles, Hoddle and Steve Perryman among those household names in the starting line-up.

We knew we had a lot of players who had not experienced this kind of thing before and I would be lying if I said that did not play on my mind, but I just had to stay focused and switched on. As far as I was concerned it was an opportunity to make my mark as an Arsenal player. I knew if I played well it would help the team's performance and increase our chances of winning.

I did not have time to get nervous because, fortunately for me, I was only told I would be playing in the team meeting, which took place on the day of the game and with just two-and-a-half hours to go until kick-off.

We did not have mobile phones back then so I could not really call any of my family to tell them the good news. I did manage to contact my mum and she was delighted for me, but she did not drive and lived too far away to make it in time for the game. It would also have been a bit scary for her in those years going to a match on her own, particularly at Spurs, so it was never an option.

Things were very different in the 1980s and it was tough because there were times when I felt different because of the colour of my skin when I was the only black player in the team or the only black person in the room. I had to just deal with it in order to get to where I wanted to in my career.

There were certain grounds I used to dread going to, Chelsea and West Ham in particular, and anywhere up north was proper bad: Leeds, Liverpool, Everton, Sunderland, Newcastle. The

Midlands were not too bad, maybe because West Brom had Laurie Cunningham, but everywhere else it was pretty strong stuff you were subjected to.

One game in particular that stands out is when we played Chelsea at Stamford Bridge, which was not the best place for a black player. I remember being racially abused by 50,000 Chelsea fans and all I could do was try to ignore it and play my game. What really shocked me was they had a black player named Paul Canoville on their bench. I remember thinking, 'Wow. If it is bad for me, imagine what it is like for him.' It must have affected him because he was just a young player trying to make his way in the game. I followed his career after that but it never really went anywhere.

The sad fact is that this kind of behaviour was accepted then and the football authorities did not do enough to stop it. I needed all the mental belief that I had and the ability to rationalise things to work my way through it. Speaking to a lot of other black players, they did the same. You cannot really fight that kind of scenario.

It was not a great situation, but if you got bitter or angry it would only have taken away from what you were trying to achieve. I look at people like Raheem Sterling and realise players now are stronger and have more power and more voice, but there is still only so much they can do.

I was the first black player to play for Arsenal for any prolonged amount of time. I did not realise then but I do now that the Caribbean community in London were following my progress and willing me on, wanting me to do well.

They were frightened of going to games because of the climate in the country, but I look at the number of black Arsenal supporters who go now and I believe that is where it started. That community felt they could connect with me and, in later years, David Rocastle and Michael Thomas.

Even now people often come up to me and say, 'We support Arsenal because of you. We did not feel comfortable going to games but we followed you.' That is so gratifying and so rewarding, knowing that is the effect people like me, Rocky and Michael had. I feel really proud.

Rocky was six years younger than me and in football terms that is a long time. He would have been a kid watching me play when I first broke into the team but, because we came from the same part of London and both had Caribbean heritage, we had a connection.

Both he and Mickey would come to me and ask for advice as I was seen as a bit of a father figure and I felt kind of responsible for them, but I knew they had the right mental attitude along with the ability to succeed. All I tried to do was support them and make sure they believed in themselves if they had a bad game or if the media were being critical of them.

Mickey was from Clapham and Rocky from Peckham, neither of which were far from my family home. We all grew up on Inner London council estates and went to the same type of schools, so there were a lot of similarities in our upbringing.

I got to know Rocky's family very well, his mum, brother and sister, and his wife and children, so our connection ran a lot deeper than football and it was the same with Mickey's family. I feel good about the time we all had together and that we all came from south London and all made it in such a tough industry. Sadly, Rocky passed away in March 2001 aged only 33 and far too young but he certainly left his mark and is still remembered as a special character and a special player.

When I made my debut the team used to meet for a pre-match brunch at South Herts Golf Club in Totteridge, not far from our London Colney training ground, and that is when Terry revealed his line-up. After listening to his game plan, we jumped on the coach to make the relatively short journey to north London.

I remember sitting on the bus with blue skies overhead and feeling really excited about the prospect of making my debut in such a big game, especially for the fans. I just tried to mentally prepare myself. When we arrived, there was a lot of activity outside the stadium with Arsenal supporters cheering as we disembarked from the coach and the Spurs faithful giving us a less friendly welcome. We did not have bricks coming through the windows or anything that bad, but could feel they were not supporting us!

I was struck by the sheer volume of people and seeing the excitement on the fans' faces made me realise even more exactly how important this game was. The atmosphere as the coach drew closer to the ground itself really started getting to me, but then your professional head kicks in. I wanted to enjoy every moment, but you only enjoy it if your team win and if you perform well as an individual so that was at the forefront of my mind.

I signed a couple of autographs before making my way down the long corridor to the away dressing room and once inside it all became eerily quiet and calm. My kit had already been hung up, all pristine with my boots laid out underneath my number eight shirt. When I ran out for the warm-up and looked around the stadium, I told myself I really had to perform well because there was so much at stake in terms of the fans and also my own career.

The match itself went by in a blur. I know we won 2-1, with Alan Sunderland coming off the subs' bench to get the winner, and it was a great feeling to beat your rivals with such a young set of players. The manager was really pleased both with the team and with my own personal performance, which gave me a lot of satisfaction.

Once the job was done, we were able to really enjoy the moment and there was a lot of laughter and hugging in our changing room before we all went into the players' lounge and had a drink and a mingle with the Tottenham players and their families, which was more commonplace then than it is now.

It was a great moment for me as I had been an avid Arsenal fan since watching Charlie George score his winner in the 1971 FA Cup Final on television. My love for the club had already taken hold, so you can imagine my excitement when I was invited for trials at Highbury aged 13 or 14.

I grew up in Stockwell and it was while playing for the South London District in the National Schools' Cup that Arsenal first spotted me. We reached the final and, as we went through the rounds, more and more scouts started to appear at our matches.

I was offered a two-year apprenticeship with Arsenal at 16, which of course I lapped up, and in those days, you trained every day but were also responsible for cleaning the changing rooms and the boots for the first-team players.

I had a mixture of boots to clean for players like Dave Price, Peter Storey, Brian Talbot, Alan Ball and Alan Hudson and it was a great experience for me, mixing with professional footballers at such a tender age.

I will always be thankful to Terry Neill for giving me my debut, but we had some tough times under him and probably did not win as many games as we should have. He had some strong characters in the changing room to deal with, people like Willie Young, who were not always easy to keep in line. Don Howe was Terry's assistant and used to do most of the training and tactical stuff. They were two different characters, who complemented each other well.

I ended up staying at Arsenal for 18 years man and boy and we had some good times, but some difficult days also. There were times, before George Graham came in as a manager, when we were not winning anything and only 13,000 people would turn up for our home games.

We were losing badly to poor teams and did not seem to be going anywhere and it was only when George arrived that he sorted it all out by getting rid of a lot of players, putting young lads in and organising us into a squad that could start challenging for honours.

George changed us into a winning machine and we had such a good togetherness in the squad and were hungry. We played some really good football and won pretty much all there was to win. Those things live with you forever and, if I was looking back, I would be saying a big well done to that 17-year-old making his way to White Hart Lane for all that he went on to achieve.

BOB WILSON

Bob Wilson
Goalkeeper
1963–1974

Bob Wilson borrowed a car to drive from Loughborough College, where he was studying to be a teacher, to join Arsenal. One chat with manager Billy Wright, and a look around the historic wonders of Highbury, and Wilson was ready to embark on a glittering career with the Gunners as a player from 1963 to 1974 and as a goalkeeping coach for 28 years until 2003. Wilson was Arsenal's keeper when they won the Double in 1970/71 (he was also player of the year) and when they won the Inter-Cities Fairs Cup in 1970. He was also the goalkeeping coach when they twice more won the Double. Chesterfield-born Wilson kept 125 clean sheets in 308 first-team appearances. Renowned for his bravery, Wilson might never have been associated with Arsenal for so long had his father, Chesterfield's Borough Engineer, not turned down overtures from Manchester United for his 16-year-old son on the basis that football was not a proper career. Wilson was twice capped by Scotland, for whom he qualified through his parents, and was a key figure in some golden years in the 70s under Bertie Mee and Don Howe. Later, he went into television, first with the BBC and later ITV, and made far more money than he ever did playing football. After the tragic death of his 31-year-old daughter Anna from a rare cancer, Wilson set up the Willow Foundation in her honour in 1999 and in 2007 was awarded the OBE. He also achieved the ultimate accolade of having a song named after him, Bob Wilson – Anchorman, by Half Man Half Biscuit. Wilson might have chosen the match of his life from any number of important games but remembers bringing a European trophy to Highbury for the first time in Arsenal's history with particular fondness.

Arsenal 3-0 Anderlecht

Inter-Cities Fairs Cup Final, second leg
Tuesday, 28 April 1970
Highbury, London
Attendance: 51,612

Arsenal	**Anderlecht**
Wilson	Trappeniers
Storey	Heylens
McNab	Martins
Kelly	Nordahl
McLintock	Velkeneers
Simpson	Kialunda
Armstrong	Desanghere
Sammels	Devrindt
Radford	Mulder
George	Van Himst
Graham	Puis

Managers

Bertie Mee   Pierre Sinibaldi

Goals

Kelly
Radford
Sammels

Nothing will ever come near the thrill of beating Tottenham to complete the Double of 1970/71 in my mind, but the win over two legs in the 1970 Inter-Cities Fairs Cup Final laid the foundations for much of the club's future success. Arsenal hadn't won anything, home nor abroad, in 17 years, which was an age for a club of that size and, to achieve it, we had to come back from a three-goal deficit. The following year we won the league and FA Cup and spent the 70s winning or nearly winning other cups and trophies, so beating this very good Belgian side was something of a watershed moment. Reaching the final was reasonably straightforward in that we saw off Glentoran, Sporting Lisbon, Rouen of France and the Romanian side, Dinamo Bacau, comfortably enough over two legs, and it was not until the semi-final, where we ran into a burgeoning Ajax side, that we encountered truly strong opposition. This young Ajax team was on the threshold of world dominance built around the extraordinary skills of Johan Cruyff, the greatest foreign player I ever played against. I had never seen a player with so many tricks and the rest of the team complemented him so that their jigsaw of rough and smooth edges was coming together. Total Football was born.

We won 3-1 on aggregate but we could see how Ajax were going to be a big team and so it proved the following year when they beat us in European competition, Peter Marinello missing a sitter, as I recall, and George Graham scoring an own goal. Later, I got to know Cruyff and his family personally – we holidayed in the same place – and he once sent me a picture of himself and said, 'What would you give for a body like that?'

And so to the final. I point to it as the completion of our own jigsaw, the one match of two legs which gave us the confidence as individuals and as a team to go on and compete for so much, so successfully in the next few years. It was about time we won something. We had lost the 1968 League Cup Final, when

I was injured and didn't play, and the 1969 League Cup Final humiliatingly to Swindon on a Wembley mud-heap. The *Daily Express* headline over Desmond Hackett's match report talked of 'The Shame of London' after the Wiltshire Third Division side had beaten us 3-1. It was impossible to play decent football on that surface but Swindon were the better team on the day and I'm not going to trot out excuses. We got a tankard each as runners-up and I remember our captain, Frank McLintock, who had lost several finals with Leicester and Arsenal, throwing his into seven inches of mud as Swindon celebrated, and shouting: 'Not another f***ing tankard.'

McLintock deserved better because he was an inspirational captain, a powerful motivator and an experienced and knowledgeable footballer, and he played a key role in the way we eventually overcame an Anderlecht side laced with Belgian internationals and a Dutchman in attack, Jan Mulder, who was the Cruyff before Cruyff, if you see what I mean. Mulder was a hugely talented player and prolific scorer. Alongside him in attack was Paul Van Himst, who was established as one of the best players in the world. It was a formidable partnership. Behind McLintock, I was the second-oldest player in the team and I think we both realised how important this final was going to be.

The first leg was at Anderlecht's Constant Vanden Stock Stadion and they overran us. Mulder scored twice and Johan Devrindt the other as they threatened to sweep us aside in a tide of brilliant, smooth football, exhilarating to watch unless you were on the end of it, as we were for 75 one-sided minutes. Then in the 77th minute Bertie Mee sent on Ray Kennedy as a substitute for Charlie George. Kennedy was a big raw striker who went on to have a fine career with ourselves and then Liverpool but at this stage he was 18 and very inexperienced. This was only his fifth appearance but he got us a goal five minutes after coming on to make the final score 3-1, away goals counting double.

We got back into the dressing room, muttering and swearing among ourselves, very much a beaten team. It was all rather quiet. We just wanted to sit there with our thoughts, shower and get on a plane to go home. Step forward Frank McLintock from the showers, full of Scottish fury, to unleash one of the most inspirational speeches I can ever remember. Frank was incandescent. He could see another runners-up tankard heading for his mantlepiece and he didn't like it one little bit. In amongst the impassioned f***ing and blinding, the message was: 'We only need to win the return leg 2-0. We can do it.' Suddenly the whole mood changed. Suddenly, one by one, the players were visibly lifted, realising the task was by no means beyond them on our own ground at Highbury. From the bleak desolation of defeat, we left that dressing room fired up for the return leg six days later. It was an incredible transformation and all down to Frank's spectacular invective, spoken from the heart. I liken it to the film *Braveheart*; the same Scottish passion and determination.

This went on all through the week building to the second leg. Frank kept up the momentum, instilling in us all the belief that we could overcome this two-goal deficit. Anderlecht were good but we just felt this was going to be our night.

I will never forget that April evening at Highbury. There were more than 51,000 packed into the wonderful old stadium and the noise they made was extraordinary, absolutely incredible. They drove us on, through the deep mud and into the heart of the opposition. Eddie Kelly, our Scottish midfield player, pulled a goal back midway through the first half with a shot from the edge of the area but, at the interval, for all our pressure, we were still 3-2 down on aggregate. A long way to go.

Anderlecht were not the team they had been in the first leg, although they could have put the game beyond us soon after the resumption, a shot from Van Himst hitting a post and rebounding to me. Then with about 15 minutes to go and the crowd roaring us on, Bob McNab got down the left and crossed deep to the far post where John Radford rose above the defence to score with a downward header. The whole place took off. I had never heard noise like it and you could see, in contrast, Anderlecht shoulders and heads dropping. Seconds later, a cross-field pass from Charlie George eluded the Belgian left-back and Jon Sammels smashed home a low shot into the corner. Mayhem ensued.

People say today that it was the greatest game ever played at Highbury and, for the ferocity of the crowd alone, it's hard to see how it could have been bettered.

At the final whistle, fans poured on to the pitch. It was bedlam. The Anderlecht goalkeeper, Jean-Marie Trappeniers, asked to swap shirts and I did, but when I looked at his meagre Fred Perry offering in this exchange deal I decided not to put it on. I didn't like the look of it, so on our laps of honour I decided I would prefer to be bare chested. Halfway round, one of my team-mates said he was going to the sanctuary of the dressing room because a full-scale pitch invasion looked probable. But not me. I made sure I enjoyed every second of this adulation. I had come a long way: this amateur schoolteacher, as I was occasionally referred to, had negotiated a tortuous path from England schoolboys, the Manchester United experience, to Wolves Reserves and physical training college and I wasn't going to let this glorious moment slip past unacknowledged.

When we did all return to the dressing room, Bertie Mee gave a Churchillian speech about how huge this win was for Arsenal, and his number two, Don Howe, said it was not so much the end of a long campaign but the beginning of a whole new era, and he was right. It was. The following year we did the Double and throughout the next decade we were one of the strongest teams in Europe.

It was Mee who played an intrinsic part in me joining Arsenal. He had spotted me playing for the British Universities team and recommended me to Billy Wright, describing me in less than flattering terms as 'crackers'. This was because of my penchant for diving headfirst at the feet of forwards, but, after I had driven down in that borrowed car to Highbury to meet Mr Wright, I fell in love with Arsenal instantly: the marble halls, the bust of Herbert Chapman – that great manager of the 30s – the dressing rooms, the pitch. There was an aura about the place, the awe-inspiring history and the feeling of tradition, making it more like a church than a football ground. When the time came for the club to leave Highbury and move to the Emirates Stadium it made sense economically but it was a wrench for those players like me who had so loved the place. Arsene Wenger said it broke his heart and Thierry Henry said he understood why it meant so much to us.

Even further back, as a 16-year-old I wanted to sign for Manchester United. I was a schoolboy international team-mate of Nobby Stiles and trained with United, meeting all those wonderful players who died in February 1958 in the Munich air crash. Matt Busby offered me the chance but my father felt with justification that I needed qualifications and turned it down on my behalf. Years later, after Arsenal had beaten United, I was chatting with Stiles when Busby appeared in the corridor. Busby jokingly said he didn't want to talk to any opponent who had just beaten his team but then Stiles asked him if he remembered me. Busby took a look and then said: 'Ah, the boy whose father wouldn't allow him to sign for us.' Maybe my father had a point. Football was not an especially well-paid job in those days. I would have earned more as a teacher. In fact, my first wage was £30 a week, and the year we won the Double with win and draw bonuses over 64 competitive games my salary was £17,000 for the year. But what a way to make a living. There were times when I had to pinch myself to think I had got to that level. It was a great privilege and one I never took for granted.

ANDERS LIMPAR

Anders Limpar
Midfielder
1990–1994

Anders Limpar arrived at Highbury from Cremonese in the summer of 1990, an exciting Swedish international winger who had made a big impression in the tough world of Serie A before his £1m transfer. Limpar was in for a bit of a culture shock as the only foreigner in a British dressing room but soon adapted and went on to score 20 goals in 116 league and cup appearances. Limpar left Arsenal after an acrimonious split with manager George Graham four years later but departed for Everton in a £1.6m deal with a bag full of medals: the league in 1991, the League Cup and FA Cup in 1993 and the European Cup Winners' Cup in 1994, although by the time the Gunners beat Parma in the final, Limpar had already departed for Goodison Park. After four years at Everton, Limpar returned home to Sweden and was the intended victim of an outrageous prank by Swedish TV in which they tried to convince him he had been propelled forward two years in a time machine. Even his dog was in on the ruse. Here he goes back nearly 30 years rather than forward, recounting the final match of the 1990/91 season and the only hat-trick of his senior career.

Arsenal 6-1 Coventry
Division One
Saturday, 11 May 1991
Highbury, London
Attendance: 41,039

Arsenal
Seaman
Dixon
Adams
Bould
Winterburn
Davis
Hillier
Limpar
Merson (Linighan)
Campbell (Groves)
Smith

Coventry
Ogrizovic
Borrows
Sansom (Edwards)
Peake
Pearce
Emerson
Gynn
Smith
Woods
Gallacher
Regis

Managers

George Graham   Terry Butcher

Goals

Peake (OG)   Gallacher
Limpar (3)
Smith
Groves

To be fair to Coventry and to put the match in perspective, we had already been crowned champions after beating Manchester United at Highbury, so there was no pressure. But we wanted to win for its own sake. The trophy was going to be presented to us after the game whatever the result and we knew Highbury would be packed with our supporters desperate to enjoy a festive occasion. We wanted to beat Coventry in style for them. George Graham acknowledged that we had been involved in a long, hard season and gave us a week off leading up to the visit of the Sky Blues. One or two of the players went away but I stayed in London and relaxed my muscles ready for one last push.

Highbury was indeed almost full and there was an air of expectancy. Coventry made it a little easy for us, leaving big gaps at the back which we were able to exploit. The first goal, put into his own net at full stretch by the diving Trevor Peake, set us on our way and from then on the result was never in doubt. My first goal followed later, Kevin Campbell flicking on a long kick down field by David Seaman and I finished it with a nice right-foot shot, low into the corner. Coventry pulled one back but then Alan Smith got his 27th of the season. At 3-1 we knew we had won.

I have to say Alan Smith was the best forward I ever played with. There was a calmness about him, an ability to sort of suck the ball into his body so that he never lost it under pressure. He was like a magnet and a key man in our strategy, which was to get the ball to him and move when he laid it off, often to me on the wing. You always knew that if you were able to get forward and get a cross into the opposition box, Alan would be there to contest it. We had a strong side when I was there but Alan was crucial to us and I often think he was underrated; people didn't realise just how good a player he was.

My second goal owed much to the powerful running of Kevin Campbell, who burst clear of a square defence and looked as if he was about to finish it off himself. But the Coventry goalkeeper,

Steve Ogrizovic, was a big man and he didn't commit himself as Kevin bore down on him, which made him go wide. Kevin showed great composure, refused to panic and laid the ball perfectly into my path. With my left foot I was able to score from about five yards, my shot eluding a couple of defenders on the line. I was pleased with that one.

Lee Dixon put me away for my third and our fifth. His left-foot clearance found a big hole in the Coventry defence, I shrugged off an intended tackle and, with the goalkeeper blocking my way, was able to place my shot past him.

At this stage, the crowd were chanting 'Super Swede' from all sides of the stadium, as they had done from the day I arrived. I had a great rapport with the Arsenal fans and I can't tell you how honoured I felt by the way they took me to their hearts as one of their own. It was always an amazing, spine-tingling feeling hearing them call me Super Swede and it helped me settle in my new surroundings from the very start. I can only thank them for being so kind.

In fact, my whole Arsenal experience was wonderful. Joining Arsenal was the best thing I ever did and I had an unbelievable four years at Highbury. I feel blessed with the good fortune to have played in one of the best club sides ever produced, not just at Arsenal but by any team. Not only that, but they were all nice guys, all good men. When I arrived from Italy, I found myself the only foreigner, and it could have been awkward and difficult. I had to adapt to them, their way of doing things and their whole way of life. Not many Swedes or Danes had made much of an impression on the world stage and here I was, a little winger from Cremonese none of them knew anything about. It was very strange. None of them had heard of me or knew anything of my background. They just knew I was a Swedish international winger, nothing more. But they quickly made me part of the squad and never once did I feel like an outsider.

There was no getting away from the fact that the football was very different from that played in Italy. At the time, I must say Serie A was much better that the Football League. In Italy the game was more thoughtful, considered and skilful. But in England it was twice as quick and that was a shock to the system because I had never experienced anything like it. The pace was unbelievable, you never got time to think, and, to be honest, I liked that. The football was exciting and fast and it suited my game. The crowds wanted you to 'have a go', get forward and attack.

The Arsenal lads could not have been more helpful. Guys like Paul Merson, Michael Thomas, Dixon, David Rocastle and others went out of their way to help me settle in London and at Arsenal. Alan Smith even came with me to help me find a home to buy. For someone new to a big city, as I was, finding a house could be a bit daunting but Alan spent the day with me – a great act of kindness. And then there was Brian Marwood, the winger I had been signed to replace. Brian was an absolute gentleman who gave such a valuable insight into the way Arsenal played, what I would be expected to contribute and lots of valuable advice. I can't forget that.

But then, we had a great team. Few stood out more than Tony Adams, our captain. He was the best captain of a team I ever played in by far. Tony wasn't a ranter on the pitch. He led by outstanding example. In fact, he was silent on the pitch but in the dressing room he let you know if he thought you were not doing your job. We all responded to his leadership; we all looked up to him.

Anyway, returning to my match, Perry Groves, on as a substitute, got the sixth from a centre by Nigel Winterburn and a few moments later, to the spray of champagne and fireworks, we were being presented with the league trophy and parading it around our jubilant supporters. It had been quite a season, my first in England, and we now had time to reflect on some of the highlights – and lowlights.

For me, scoring my first goal in English football against Chelsea on a counter-attack was a bit of a landmark. I had gone about six games since my arrival without getting on the scoresheet and was becoming a little anxious. I needed a goal. I think it came from a long ball up to Smith and I finished off the move with a low shot. I can recall the relief. To score my first goal at Highbury was important and to get it against a quality side like Chelsea confirmed in my own mind that I could live with the best.

The other big moment of that season – and bearing in mind we lost only once – came at Old Trafford and the infamous mass brawl in which I'm sorry to say I played an important part. I remember the match being so hard and physical and I was struggling to adapt. Both ourselves and Manchester United were high in the table, so there was a lot at stake.

Anyway, it all started when United forward Brian McClair kicked Nigel Winterburn in the back as he lay on the ground. I responded in support of my stricken team-mate by punching McClair and all hell broke loose with virtually every player on both sides getting involved in the brawl and the managers, George Graham and Alex Ferguson, hurling insults at each other on the touchline. I didn't get a red card, but might have done, and in fact no one was sent off. Instead the FA hit us hard by depriving us of two points and United of one. I was one of four Arsenal players fined by the club and, while I can't complain, I think we might all have been fined. It was an incredible scene. In retrospect, I think this was the match that first sparked the intense rivalry between Arsenal and Manchester United that would continue for many seasons.

That first year was outstanding for me with 13 league and cup goals and, in my second year, fans might remember me scoring from 40 yards with a shot which found the Liverpool goalkeeper Mike Hooper off his line, but my appearances and contributions became fewer as time went on. I got medals for the cup Double win of 1993 without playing in either final and the club were decent enough to send me a Cup Winners' Cup medal after I had moved to Everton. I had played in earlier matches.

To be honest, I think the manager became a little more cautious over my last year or two. When I first arrived, we were a top-class counter-attacking team, ahead of our time, but I suffered from his desire to play an extra defender on occasions. I don't know why he became scared in that way, because we had been very successful in the past and didn't need to change tactics.

At the end of my four-year contract I asked George for another four years but he told me he could not guarantee me a place and that it was best I left. He told me that he was selling me to Manchester City and I said that I didn't want to go there. I wanted to stay because I had had such a good time at Arsenal. I would have liked to have stayed for ten years.

But there was no changing George's mind and I'm afraid that, as a result of our conversation, I left on a bad note.

I didn't go to Manchester City. I went instead to Everton, the club of my childhood, and won the FA Cup with them in 1995, the standout moment during four great years at Goodison Park.

But I look back on my time with Arsenal with huge affection. I still meet some of my ex-colleagues when I come back to England and we talk about the great days and the great matches. Above all, as I say, I was extremely fortunate to have played for one of Arsenal's best, best teams.

JOHN JENSEN

John Jensen
Midfielder
1992–1996

The epitome of an Arsenal cult hero, John Jensen was born in the Danish capital Copenhagen and enjoyed two spells at Brondby with a fleeting stay at German side Hamburg sandwiched in between. The midfielder shot to prominence by scoring a superb solo goal in Denmark's shock 1992 European Championship Final win over Germany. The Danes had failed to qualify for the tournament before being called off the beach as 11th-hour replacements when war-ravaged Yugoslavia were forced to pull out. Jensen's performances throughout the competition persuaded George Graham to bring him to Highbury for a fee of in excess of £1m, making him part of the Premier League's original foreign legion. Jensen helped Arsenal complete the domestic cup Double in his first season before tasting European Cup Winners' Cup glory in his home city the following year. Famously, Jensen only ever managed one goal in 138 competitive games for the club before returning to Denmark in 1996. Jensen's coaching career included a stint as assistant manager to Steve Kean at Blackburn Rovers.

Arsenal 1-3 Queens Park Rangers

Premier League
Saturday, 31 December 1994
Highbury, London
Attendance: 32,393

Arsenal	QPR
Bartram	Roberts
Dixon	Wilson
Bould	Bardsley
Keown	McDonald
Winterburn	Maddix
Jensen	Hodge
Schwarz	Meaker
Parlour	Barker
Wright	Impey
Smith (Clarke)	Gallen
Campbell	Ferdinand (Allen)

Managers
George Graham — Ray Wilkins

Goals
Jensen	Gallen
	Allen
	Impey

JOHN JENSEN

Like many former footballers, I have a room in my house where I keep the most treasured mementos from my playing career. There you will find the Denmark jersey I wore to victory in the European Championships, as well as my shirts from the FA Cup Final and Cup Winners' Cup Final wins with Arsenal. They were all the best of days.

Also taking pride of place among my collection of memorabilia is the T-shirt Arsenal produced with 'I was there when John Jensen scored' emblazoned across it. That shows just how much that moment, 98 games in the making, meant to me and I very much regard it as a badge of honour.

I remember going to the club shop a couple of days after the game and asking if I could have one of the T-shirts but they had completely sold out and had to print another one especially for me, so anybody who still has one can legitimately say they are in possession of a collector's item.

What I did not know when I signed for Arsenal was that the fans were asking the club for a midfield player who could create chances and score goals, having just agreed to sell David Rocastle to Leeds. I could do both of those things but not with the regularity they wanted.

I was not a Liam Brady, I wish I was, but George Graham wanted a hardworking midfielder to sit in front of his famous back four of Lee Dixon, Tony Adams, Steve Bould and Nigel Winterburn and protect them.

When people talk about that legendary defence, I think I was part of it because Tony and Steve Bould were on my back all the time during games, ordering me to sit there and do the hard work. I felt that was my job.

I could still play good passes forward to Ian Wright and did have a lot of shots, so never did I imagine it would take me nearly 100 games to score a goal. In a way that was not good but at the same time it was good, because the fans found out what type of player I was and the respect I got from them was absolutely huge, hence the popularity of the T-shirt.

If I had been playing in Italy and had racked up 30 games in my first season without scoring, they would probably have booed me, but the Arsenal supporters always applauded and encouraged me. Whenever I met one of them, they would say, 'We know you are working your bollocks off for the team', and they liked that.

Despite my lack of goals, I was never afraid to respond to the fans' calls of 'shoooot'. I remember in the semi-final of the Cup Winners' Cup against Paris St Germain being so convinced I had scored that I actually raised both hands above my head ready to celebrate. Our French opponents had the tracksuit-bottom wearing Bernard Lama in goal and I noticed he was quite a long way off his line, around about the penalty spot. I was 30 yards out so I looped the ball over the top of Lama towards the top corner only for him to race back to his unguarded goal and jump like a puma to somehow tip the ball with his fingernails on to the post and over the crossbar. No other goalkeeper in the world would have made that save and what he did with his jump was unbelievable.

That was as close as I came to scoring before the QPR game during which I had two fantastic shots in the first half and was certain both were heading for the corner only for their goalkeeper, Tony Roberts, who later joined the coaching staff at Arsenal, to make a couple of tremendous saves. That gave me a lot of confidence as I really believed after that, that it was destined to be my day and knew I was hitting the ball really well every time I came forward.

For my long-awaited goal, Nigel Winterburn got the ball down the left-hand side and I offered myself in support. He passed the ball back to me and after running quite a long way with it I just thought 'Why not finish it?', because I had that good feeling from my near misses in the first half. I hit it at three quarters of my usual pace, like a golfer taking a bit off his back swing, and watched the ball curl towards the top corner of the goal. I knew straight away this one, this time, was going in.

I had spoken a lot with my team-mates about what we would do when I scored as we used to joke about the fact I never had and I remember Kevin Campbell and Ian Wright saying they would carry me on their shoulders all the way back to the halfway line, but when it actually happened we totally forgot about all of those conversations.

All the other Arsenal players just crowded around me in front of the North Bank and I was very happy the goal went in at that end of the ground where the most hard-core and noisiest fans used to be situated. I could see in the eyes of not just the supporters but also my team-mates that it meant a lot to them all, as well as me.

The only disappointing thing was that we lost the game but that did not seem to matter. It was a great goal, on New Year's Eve, the last day of 1994, and when they were leaving the ground, I could hear people chanting my name. It was like we had just won the FA Cup all over again. They were standing up and singing my song and it seemed to mean more than the result that they had seen me score and witnessed a moment of history.

As a team we were not especially bad in that game, but were not good either. It was an average performance and normally after a defeat George Graham would come into the dressing room, have a go at us and tell us how useless we had been. This time he just said, 'JJ, congratulations on a great goal. Happy New Year everybody and I will see you all on Monday.'

George's post-match team talk felt as quick as my move to north London, and it was a week after winning the European Championship Final against Germany that my club Brondby told me there was some interest from Italy, France and England. Then suddenly, the chairman called me and said I needed to take a flight the next day because I was going to sign for Arsenal!

Arsenal was not one of the names I had heard about being interested in me so I was in shock but also very, very happy, so I got myself booked on the first flight I could. I said to myself, 'Oh my God.' Arsenal were one of the biggest clubs in England and they wanted to sign me. I was absolutely over the moon.

The next day I met George and Managing Director Ken Friar at Highbury. It was a good meeting and they showed me the famous marble halls and told me a little bit about the history of the club.

I had my medical and signed a contract that afternoon before flying back to Copenhagen to collect all my belongings in the evening. It all happened very fast because there was no doubt in my mind that as soon as the chairman told me Arsenal were interested I was going to sign for them.

I had loved English football since I was a four-year-old boy and would always watch the FA Cup Final and one televised game every Saturday with my dad and grandad. I had played in Germany and, when I went back to Denmark, I told myself I really wanted to try and get to England so it could not have been any better; it was like a dream come true.

My arrival coincided with the advent of the Premier League. I did not really realise what that meant because it did not matter to me what the league was called – Division One or the Premier League – it was still the number one league in England and the best in the world.

Later on, I realised that it was special because I was one of only 13 foreign players who took part in the very first round of fixtures. The others were my team-mate Anders Limpar, the Manchester United trio of Eric Cantona, Peter Schmeichel and Andrei Kanchelskis, the Norwegian Gunnar Halle, Ronny Rosenthal of Liverpool, Manchester City's Michel Vonk, Roland Nilsson – a

Swedish right-back at Sheffield Wednesday – and goalkeepers Craig Forrest, Jan Stejskal and Hans Segers. The select list was completed by Robert Warzycha, a pacy Polish winger who turned out briefly for Everton.

The dressing room I walked into was virtually entirely made up of British players, but straight away I was made to feel welcome. I came from a dressing room at Brondby that was very similar to Arsenal's and they took good care of me.

From the start I just tried to be myself and quickly became part of a group that must have been one of the best in England with the personalities they had and the manager. The whole dressing room was together, it was perfect.

Tony Adams was the captain and then there were people like Wrighty, Steve Bould, Ray Parlour, Nigel Winterburn and David Seaman. I cannot say a bad word about anyone because everybody was fantastic. Pat Rice was the youth-team coach and he was brilliant too, an absolutely amazing man. He was always asking me how I was settling in and making sure I was okay; it was one big family.

I see some of them more than others these days but when we do get together there is always plenty of laughter. I interviewed Wrighty when I was working for Danish television and the banter was there straight away. It was like we were going back 20 years.

A lot of clubs at that time had a bit of a drinking culture and we were no different. I enjoyed that side of things, hanging out and socialising with my new team-mates, which also helped me settle in. I very much enjoyed the English humour and it was suited to me.

In my first year we won the cup Double, becoming the first team ever to win the League Cup and FA Cup in the same season, beating Sheffield Wednesday in both finals. To come to a big club and make history in that way was beyond my wildest dreams.

I was still basking in the glow of Denmark's unexpected triumph at the Euros, and there I was, standing at the old Wembley holding aloft the trophy after the longest match in FA Cup Final history. We had won it in the 119th minute, which was an incredible feeling.

We had drawn the first game six days earlier 1-1 and taken an early lead in the replay through Wrighty only for David Hirst to equalise and ensure the match went to extra time. When Andy Linighan came up from defence to get the winner with virtually the last play of the game it was a fantastic moment and I remember thinking to myself, 'Is it really true we are going to win this one?'

I will not say I got an assist for the winning goal but can claim to have had a hand in it. I picked up the ball outside the penalty area in a similar position to where I had scored for my country in the European Championship Final and I hit my shot so well that I thought it might have been going in. It struck someone on the back, went behind and Linighan headed in from the resulting corner, so I will say it was half an assist as, if I had not had the shot, then we would not have scored.

When you win a major tournament with a small country like Denmark nothing can beat it. That was absolutely top drawer. But winning the FA Cup came very close to matching the achievement because I had grown up watching countless finals back home in Scandinavia. It is a memory that makes up a big part of what I consider a magical career with the Arsenal.

I did not know until being interviewed for this book that in a poll asking Gunners fans to nominate their top ten cult heroes I came out as number two, ahead of Charlie George, Kanu and Jens Lehmann and only behind my captain Tony Adams. What a list that is and what an honour it is to feature so prominently.

I guess in that respect it was a good thing I did not score in my first 97 games for the club, because it means that goal on that afternoon stood out even more.

KEVIN CAMPBELL

Kevin Campbell
Forward
1988–1995

Lambeth-born Kevin Campbell holds the unfortunate distinction of scoring the most Premier League goals of any Englishman not to be capped by the Three Lions. Campbell signed schoolboy forms with his beloved Arsenal as a 15-year-old and was part of the Gunners' 1988 FA Youth Cup-winning team, once scoring 59 times in a single youth season. Campbell was a key man in the 1991 title success, including scoring eight goals in a blistering ten-match spell, before seeing the arrival of then-record signing Ian Wright consigning him to the fringes of the first team. Campbell fought back to play a crucial part in the League Cup and FA Cup Double win of 1992/93, claiming invaluable strikes against Millwall and Derby en route to Wembley glory, and also featured in the European Cup Winners' Cup triumph the following year. After leaving Highbury, Campbell went on to achieve cult hero status with both Nottingham Forest and Everton, whom he helped to a miracle relegation escape in 1999. But it is his time in north London that Campbell regards most fondly.

Arsenal 2-1 Sheffield Wednesday

FA Cup Final replay
Thursday, 20 May 1993
Wembley, London
Attendance: 62,267

Arsenal	Sheffield Wednesday
Seaman	Woods
Dixon	Nilsson
Adams	Anderson (Hyde)
Linighan	Warhurst
Winterburn	Worthington
Davis	Waddle (Bart-Williams)
Jensen	Palmer
Merson	Harkes
Campbell	Sheridan
Wright (O'Leary)	Hurst
Smith	Bright

Managers

George Graham	Trevor Francis

Goals

Wright	Waddle
Linighan	

The FA Cup has a long history of making heroes out of the most unlikely of players and not many people would have had money on Andy Linighan getting the winning goal in the last seconds of extra time to clinch the domestic cup Double.

I can still hear him proudly telling us in the big Wembley changing room after our dramatic victory: 'Yes, it was me who got the winner in the cup final!' Andy had such a dry sense of humour and was a great guy. I really liked him and got on with him so it could not have happened to a more deserving person.

Andy had a bit of a topsy-turvy time when he first came to Arsenal and got a bit of stick from the fans because they were not sure about him. Then, he started to play better, started to understand the system and it all culminated in his big moment at the home of football.

As a lifelong Arsenal fan, I always dreamt of playing for my team and lifting the FA Cup at Wembley so to do it for real was absolutely amazing and still feels surreal, even after reaching the age of 50.

My first trophy for the club I always loved was the league championship in 1991 and to do that at 21 you think you have died and gone to heaven but, having got the taste for it, I wanted more.

By the time the 1992/93 season came around we had made the transition from being a league-winning side to a cup-winning one. Being league champions automatically means you have a target on your back so it is so hard to keep winning more titles year after year.

We had a titanic tussle with Millwall in one of the early rounds of the League Cup, which went to penalties and I scored in the shoot-out.

That was a nice moment, to go there and win, because being a south London boy I used to train at Millwall back in the day and a lot of my mates were Millwall fans. George Graham was their former manager so it was a bit of a needle match all round.

In the cups it does not matter who scores, the key is just about getting through to the next round and we became good at that. One of the qualities of that team was we knew how to see a game out if we had something to hold on to. We had such a formidable defence in those days and I should know because I still have the scars from facing them every day in training to prove it.

I also have a recollection of David O'Leary telling us during the season that the FA Cup was such a difficult competition to win. He was right because a couple of years earlier we had lost to Tottenham in the semi-final when we were winning the league at a canter and really fancied our chances of going all the way. We played our great rivals again in the semi-final in 1993 and this time we got payback with Tony Adams scoring the only goal. That was a great feeling.

We were familiar with our cup final opponents, having already beaten Sheffield Wednesday 2-1 in the League Cup Final, when our winning goal scorer Steve Morrow ended up in hospital after being dropped on his shoulder by Tony Adams during the frantic celebrations.

To play the same team in both domestic cup finals was a real one-off and Wednesday had a good, strong, solid side with players like Mark Bright, Paul Warhurst, Carlton Palmer and Nigel Worthington so we expected it to be a battle, and it was.

After drawing 1-1 in the original tie, the replay finished with the same score after 90 minutes, with Ian Wright putting us ahead in both games only for Wednesday to twice equalise. We were maybe expecting penalties but never gave up, kept pushing and, in the end, Andy came up trumps.

The replay was a midweek game and was a fantastic night. The communal bath was still part of the Wembley dressing rooms at the time so we had a few beers in there along with the obligatory post-match pictures.

My dad and my brother had come to the game; my mum came on the Saturday but could not make the midweek match, but she still had my medal as she was a massive part of my career. After getting changed from my muddy kit into my suit, I went up and saw my family before jumping back on the team coach to join the rest of the players for a night on the town. There were Arsenal fans all over the place enjoying their celebrations, so it was a great night all round.

The whole squad had played their part in what we had achieved and under George Graham everybody knew their roles. I was the foil for Ian Wright and it was my job to be able to hold the ball up and bring others into play. I had to do that because otherwise I would not have been on the pitch for very long.

I always knew I would be a number nine because I loved scoring goals, even as a young kid growing up in Brixton when my first knowledge of football came from my dad telling me stories about Pele and Clyde Best, the former West Ham striker.

After that, Cyrille Regis was my hero because, being from south London, he was someone I could really relate to, but my first love was Arsenal and going to watch Frank Stapleton play in 1977 was something special to me, although my favourite player at the time was Liam Brady.

As a youngster I played all over the pitch most of the time but always had a knack for scoring goals. You have to be a team player as a number nine and let other people score as well as you, but to be considered a good one, you have to be able to put the ball into the back of the net.

I used to train at four or five different clubs. Fred Ricketts scouted me for Arsenal and very quickly after being scouted I met up with the legend that is Pat Rice, who used to coach the academy boys. That was a very good progression into the club.

They probably saw someone who was good and could play but needed to develop as well and someone who was coachable.

My favourite strike partner was Alan Smith, because he taught me so much about being a striker and how to play the number nine to a different level. He really brought my game on leaps and bounds.

I broke into the team before Ian Wright came to the club and had just won my first title and picked up an injury in pre-season when Arsenal brought him in. I quickly found myself out of the team because Wrighty was our record signing and he and Smith were both fully fledged England internationals.

I was the youngest of the three of us so was always going to be the one to make way, but I had two choices: either to start banging on the manager's door or get back on the training pitch with Stewart Houston, George 'Geordie' Armstrong and Pat Rice to start learning and developing my game, and that is what I did.

I had to convince the manager that I needed to start matches because I had attributes that the likes of Smith did not; things like physicality, pace and power.

Smith was strong and could lead the line very well but did not have the pace, power and directness I did. Arsenal's game was getting quicker with Ian Wright up there because the style of play was becoming more suited to his game than how we played as a team.

I knew I had to become better at holding the ball up and better at leading the line, because I needed to be able to do some of the bits and pieces Smith could. We were mates, but professional football is all about competition and we all wanted to play. There were times when I would find myself out of the team and other times when Smudge would be. George kept us on our toes very well.

At a club like Arsenal there is always going to be someone breathing down your neck and wanting that shirt and if you cannot handle that, you should not be playing top-level football.

George was brilliant to work with, an amazing coach and an amazing man. He was always teaching and therefore I was always learning and he was not afraid to play me in a lot of different positions. He was a fantastic man manager.

The season after we did the cup Double I scored 14 goals in all competitions as we won the European Cup Winners' Cup by beating Parma in the final on a brilliant night in Copenhagen.

It really clicked for me that year because it was the first time that Ian Wright and I had played together for a significant amount of time. George had pulled me to one side when Wrighty first arrived and said he did not think we could play together and that stunned me a bit at the time.

It is true the dynamic of the team changed after Wrighty's arrival from Crystal Palace because, whereas before the goals had been shared out, now he was getting the bulk of the chances. Alan Smith definitely suffered as a result of that.

It all changed for me against Sheffield Wednesday, ironically, when we beat them 7-1. Wrighty and I both started and the pair of us ran riot. That game was really what pushed the partnership together. Suddenly, I was playing every game and when you are playing every game your confidence goes up, so that was good management.

I left Arsenal because it seemed to me the George Graham era was being broken up. Chris Kiwomya and Glenn Helder had been brought in and John Hartson as well. John was a good lad and a good player and I knew Chris from the past, but there were a lot of changes gradually taking place. Dennis Bergkamp also came in the summer I left.

I don't have regrets, though. I feel pleased to have won the trophies I did for my boyhood team.

BOBBY GOULD

Bobby Gould
Forward
1968–1970

Coventry-born Bobby Gould left his home city club aged 22 to join Arsenal in the first of many moves as a player and later as a manager. Rolling stone Gould spent two years with the Gunners before signing for Wolves and then went on to play for West Bromwich Albion, Bristol City, West Ham, Wolves again, Bristol Rovers, Norwegian club Aalesunds and finally Hereford. A bustling, aggressive striker, Gould scored 179 league and cup goals in English football in 408 matches and he should know because he kept a record of every game he played in, including for the reserves. As a manager he was no less permanent, bossing Chelsea on a caretaker basis, Bristol Rovers twice, Coventry twice, Wimbledon, West Brom, Cardiff, Cheltenham and Weymouth. He was also in charge of the Welsh international squad for four years from 1995. As a manager, Gould will be remembered for being Wimbledon's ecstatic leader on the day the Crazy Gang beat the Culture Club of Liverpool 1-0 at Wembley in 1988, one of the FA Cup's biggest-ever upsets. But he was also on the receiving end of a Wembley shock when Arsenal lost to Third Division Swindon in the League Cup Final of 1969. The memory has left its scars.

Arsenal 1-3 Swindon

League Cup Final
Saturday, 15 March 1969
Wembley, London
Attendance: 98,189

Arsenal	Swindon
Wilson	Downsborough
Storey	Butler
McNab	Thomas
McLintock	Burrows
Ure	Harland
Simpson (Graham)	Trollope
Radford	Heath
Sammels	Smart
Court	Smith (Penman)
Gould	Noble
Armstrong	Rogers

Managers

Bertie Mee	Danny Williams

Goals

Gould	Smart
	Rogers (2)

As a player you dream of playing at Wembley. We all do. So, when we got through to the final of the League Cup after disposing of our great rivals Tottenham over two legs, we longed for the big day. As a lad fresh from Coventry, this was going to be my greatest moment in football. But then we had a terrible shock. On the Thursday before the match, Bertie Mee and Don Howe took us to Wembley to get a feel of the place and I will never forget my first sight of that famous pitch. As we came down the tunnel towards it, there was not the usual immaculate greensward we had a right to expect, but a soggy, boggy quagmire. I cried. Literally, I cried. And I was not alone. By all accounts the Horse of the Year Show had just taken place and the drains underneath had been damaged by the hooves of the competitors. Diabolical, absolutely diabolical. Our morale slumped as we stared at the mud and the puddles because it was not far off being unplayable. The silence among us was deafening. Bertie tried to lift us by saying it didn't matter, our greater class would tell against Third Division opponents, no matter how bad the surface. Trouble was, we knew that if the pitch was still in this terrible state at the weekend, it would favour the less skilful team and, of course, it did.

We didn't know much about Swindon. We did know they had taken 11 matches to reach the final, including three in the semi-final against Burnley, and we had been warned they had a tough and experienced line-up who were not to be underestimated. They also had, in Don Rogers, one of the great talents of his generation, a winger of classic skills and balance. Why he was still playing in the Third Division was not clear because he was worthy of a bigger stage. He was their danger man. But until that fateful visit to Wembley, we were confident – without being complacent – that we would prove to be the better side.

Our journey to the final had been much less tortuous. We received a bye in the first round, beat Sunderland 1-0 in the second and then overcame Scunthorpe 6-1 in the third. In those days you could, as a centre-forward, ruffle up the opposing goalkeeper and I barged theirs over the line to claim a goal. Today, I would have been booked at the very least.

A strange thing happened to me that day at the Old Showground. When I was at school in Coventry, we had a teacher, a Mr Bennett, who was the strictest, most miserable man on earth, I thought at the time. As I got off the coach at Scunthorpe, there he was. I quickly moved on.

In the next round I came on as a sub in a 2-1 win over Liverpool and in the quarter-final scored once in a 5-1 triumph over Blackpool. Tottenham were desperate to beat us in the semi-final but we won 1-0 at Highbury and drew the second leg 1-1 away. Wembley, here we come.

There was one other mitigating factor for our defeat by Swindon. We had had flu in the camp and our league match the previous week had been called off because of it. The fear was that, although the players were fit again, the dreadful playing surface would eventually take a physical toll. It should not be seen as an excuse, but there were some heavy legs when the match went into extra time.

The pitch, which had been worked on in vain by the ground staff, soon cut up once we got under way. Swindon, for all their lowly status, brought hordes of fans up from Wiltshire to help create a wonderful atmosphere. Under league rules, both sides had to change from their main strip; we played in blue and yellow and Swindon in all-white and for half an hour we showed our greater quality. However, in goalkeeper Peter Downsborough, Swindon had the man of the match. He made one great save after another, principally from Jon Sammels and Bob McNab in those early stages, and there seemed no way through. The harder we tried, the worse it got, and after 35 minutes we gifted them a goal. The record books say that Ian Ure and Bob Wilson made a hash of a back pass and Roger Smart took advantage. Even then, we thought this was only a temporary setback and that we would overcome it.

But as the match drifted on, the pitch became a heap, and any kind of coherent, intelligent build-up was almost impossible. We were in despair as Swindon grew in confidence, roared on by the West Country fans, and it looked all over for us until the 86th minute. George Graham, on as a replacement, saw a shot blocked but the ball looped in the air. I read what was going to happen next from outside the area and raced into the box. For once Downsborough faltered, leaving me with an open goal from 15 yards and I headed in. I can't tell you how wonderful that feeling was, scoring at Wembley in a cup final – every boy's wish fulfilled. No one can ever take it away from me. The moment was all the better because my blind dad, Roy, a diabetic, was there in the stands and would have heard the Arsenal fans roaring. His pal, Roy Kendall, was alongside him to provide the commentary. I know he was as proud as I was. There are pictures of me running behind the goal after scoring, crying. Fans thought I was crying with joy, but actually it was because I was in great pain having been kicked in the Adam's apple by the Swindon defender Frank Burrows while attempting to clear. Frank later became a great pal.

My goal pushed the match into extra time and there was still a feeling in our camp that we would prevail, that our tired legs would see us through the last 30 minutes and that it would be Swindon who would wilt.

Step forward Don Rogers. When I look at the video of that match, I see how going into extra time, Rogers's shirt and shorts were still immaculately white, as if he had just come on. That proves how little impression he had made, but then he showed just why he was a folk hero in deepest Wiltshire. Just when we thought Swindon would crumble and falter, Rogers put them ahead just before the break and then clinched the match with a run from deep that was sheer class. There was no way back.

Rogers was an amazing player. Coupled with supreme talent he had that balance you saw only in George Best and Jimmy Greaves in my generation. Ronnie Rees, my team-mate at Coventry, had that same easy movement. Many years later at a ceremony to mark an anniversary of that match, Rogers displayed that same swagger, the lithe movement of a born athlete. You can't teach it.

At the final whistle, we had to accept that Swindon, the little Third Division club, had beaten us fairly by taking their chances. I remember one or two players, amid the inevitable sadness, saying, 'How did that happen? Why did it happen?' Both of Rogers's goals stemmed from our mistakes, not that I want to take anything away from his or his club's achievements. There were no recriminations afterwards. I was pleased with my goal but it was the beginning of the end for me in Arsenal's famous red and white.

Don Howe was implementing a pressing game, now so popular and ahead of its time, and he didn't think I could do that from the front, a great shame because I loved my time with the club.

I grew up at Arsenal, as a player and as a man. When I came down from Coventry, I was a bit of a naive country boy and hadn't realised just how big Arsenal were. It was a shock. I had cost them £90,000 – only Alun Evans at Liverpool had cost more – and I don't think I gave them value for money. Bertie decided I was not the right man and for most of the next season I was in the reserves, feeling left out and a bit sorry for myself.

In fact, I started just ten league games, without scoring; my only goal was in the Inter-Cities Fairs Cup against Glentoran. For the reserves I got 31 goals in 21 games, driven by pride and my professionalism. Arsenal wanted to get their money back and turned down a bid from Aston Villa, but in the end they cut their losses and sold me to Wolves for a £30,000 loss. It was a sad way to end, because I had two great years at Highbury and could see how Bertie and Don were gradually building the 1970/71

Double-winning side. Frank McLintock was a great captain and Jon Sammels and 'Geordie' Armstrong were terrific footballers. Geordie was particularly kind. He could see how despondent I had become and I remember once how he put his arm around me and told me it would be all right.

Many of the lads from that team are still my friends; I lived next to John Radford at New Barnet, and I worked closely with Don Howe later in management.

Later, I returned to Wembley with West Ham and was on the bench when we beat Fulham 2-0 in the FA Cup Final and, of course, I was manager of Wimbledon in 1988 when we saw off Liverpool. As opposed to a runners-up medal from that Swindon defeat, I therefore have winners' medals from two matches in which I never once stepped on to the pitch. Such is football.

SAMMY NELSON

Sammy Nelson
Defender
1966–1981

Belfast-born Sammy Nelson came to Highbury as a 16-year-old winger from his home city but became one of Arsenal's best ever left-backs in a stalwart career of almost 400 league and cup appearances. Sammy signed as a professional on his 17th birthday in 1966 and made his debut in 1969 against Ipswich. The son of an Arsenal supporter, Sammy was part of the FA Youth Cup-winning side against Sunderland, the other club who tried to sign him as a schoolboy international. The redoubtable Bob McNab stood in Nelson's way for a few years until 1971/72 when he finally became the regular left-back, holding down the position for the next decade. Sammy played in four finals for Arsenal: the FA Cups of 1978, 1979 and 1980 and the European Cup Winners' Cup defeat by Valencia, also in 1980. Arsenal won only one of those – in 1979 when Manchester United were beaten 3-2 in one of Wembley's most exciting matches, a contest to this day often referred to as the 'five-minute final' since three goals were scored between the 87th and 90th minutes. Sammy played in 51 internationals for Northern Ireland (two of them in the 1982 World Cup) and was among a large contingent of Irishmen on Arsenal's books at the time: Pat Jennings, Pat Rice, David O'Leary, Liam Brady, Frank Stapleton and John Devine. Manager Terry Neill was another. Sammy later moved to Brighton for a couple of years and was in their squad for the 1983 FA Cup Final without playing. After a stellar football career, Sammy began a whole new way of life in financial services. Still living in the Brighton area, Sammy is a regular visitor to the Emirates Stadium and vividly recalls the 1979 triumph.

Arsenal 3-2 Manchester United

FA Cup Final
Saturday, 12 May 1979
Wembley, London
Attendance: 99,219

Arsenal	Manchester United
Jennings	Bailey
Rice	Nicholl
Nelson	Albiston
Talbot	McIlroy
Young	McQueen
O'Leary	Buchan
Brady	Coppell
Sunderland	J Greenhoff
Stapleton	Jordan
Price (Walford)	Macari
Rix	Thomas

Managers
Terry Neill	Dave Sexton

Goals
Talbot	McQueen
Stapleton	McIlroy
Sunderland	

SAMMY NELSON

Losing to Ipswich in 1978 had been a bit of a blow. No excuses, but we hadn't been at full strength, many of us were not fit, and we didn't do ourselves credit. A year later it was different. We were all in good condition and, even after a long season, resolutely determined to make up for our failure 12 months before. Terry Neill, the manager, and Don Howe, our coach, took us down to a training base near Bisham Abbey for a few days to prepare for the big day, away from the pressures of fans and media, and it worked. We were relaxed and ready by the time we made our way to Wembley that warm day in May. Manchester United, managed by an old coach of mine in Dave Sexton, were favourites but we weren't worried about the pundits. In recent years we had always done well against United and the manager and coach stressed that they were more likely to fear us than we would them. Terry Neill had assembled a very solid and organised team with some great individuals.

Nobody, for instance, was better than Pat Jennings in goal and he was the last line of defence behind a strong back four of Pat Rice and myself as the full-backs and Willie Young and 21-year-old David O'Leary in the centre. In midfield, we knew Brian Talbot and David Price would always be up and down the pitch, Graham Rix had a sweet left foot and in Liam Brady we had one of the best players in the country, a player who could unlock any defence with his skill and vision. Our front two consisted of young Frank Stapleton, dynamic in the air and rapidly improving on the ground, and Alan Sunderland, a super quick forward not many defenders could catch in full flow. We knew all about our opponents, as they would have done us, but there was a feeling inside our camp that we were the better team.

And so it proved. For some odd reason, United were nervous in that first half and didn't do themselves justice. By the break we were two goals up and, had we taken another chance or two in that first 45 minutes, the game would have been over as a contest.

But two goals is never enough to be sure of success and United showed no signs of giving up. The first goal was an unusual one in that for a long time, even afterwards, no one was sure who scored it. A cross came in from the right and when the ball was swept past Gary Bailey, it could have been Talbot or Price who got the final touch. They both claimed it, as they would, but the consensus was that the goal was Talbot's. This was the perfect lift and reward for our early dominance and just before the break we got another. Brady eluded two challenges on the right and crossed with his weaker foot, his right, into the danger area where he picked out Stapleton perfectly to head in from ten yards or so. Great credit of course to Brady for opening up the United left flank like that but also to Stapleton for getting away from Martin Buchan with a clever dummy and leaving himself with time and room for an easy header. Brady was a wonderful player and on the threshold of a great career at home and abroad and we acknowledged that, in him, we had a match-winner. We never minded if he didn't chase back because he was always creating goals for others. Half-time came and we were well on top, cruising along at 2-0 and disappointed only that we were not further in front. We should have banged the final nail into their coffin.

To be honest, the second half was largely uneventful and as time ticked by there were no obvious signs of a United rally. They were working hard enough without extending us and I think we were all thinking that we just had to keep our composure and shape and we would see United off. But that all changed in those dramatic last few minutes of mayhem. United had by now, two goals down and five minutes to play, abandoned any semblance of a plan and threw men forward in a desperate last attempt to snatch a goal or two – and that's exactly what they did. There was a free kick on the right and we should have cleared it, but it ricocheted around – or so it seemed to me at the time – in our area and Gordon McQueen prodded home. Surely this was just a consolation. There were only four minutes left and it would have been a massive shock if United, after doing nothing for so long, now came back to equalise. I remember thinking how we were in for a very tough few minutes because this goal would have given them a big lift.

Two minutes later they got another. Another Irishman, Sammy McIlroy, almost stumbled his way through a couple of challenges and, although Rice tried to get to him, he managed to steer a shot past Jennings as the goalkeeper dived at his feet in vain. Suddenly it's 2-2 and the noise was phenomenal. United's fans, so subdued for most of the afternoon, were in full voice and our supporters, doubtlessly shocked by the late twist in events, were just as raucous in trying to revive us, so that the atmosphere going into the last minute of the match was simply incredible.

In amongst all this chaos, I remember two moments, the first of them almost surreal, as United, jubilant at their tremendous recovery, made their way back to the kick-off. I remember looking up at the royal box and thinking I should have been going up there in the next couple of minutes to get my winner's medal but now it would not be happening. The second I will never be able to explain to myself. I spotted a divot, kicked out of this flawless playing surface, and carefully replaced it like a golfer might on a green, making sure it fitted neatly back into its position. I suppose I was just reflecting on the sharp turn in events, because we all had to prepare mentally as well as physically for extra time. None of us saw this happening.

I can recall Brian Greenhoff getting ready to come on for United as a substitute with extra time seconds away as we kicked off again, still dazed by the turn of events, but within seconds we had scored the winner. I was involved in the move initially, as was Stapleton, before Brady fed Rix on the left and his centre drifted over Bailey and Arthur Albiston, the left-back, for Sunderland to rush the ball over the line at the far post. Incredible; no other word.

Wembley erupted. Our fans, still reeling from those late United goals, were ecstatic and the whole United portion of a 100,000 crowd were plunged into silence, seconds after wildly celebrating. It had to be seen to be believed, the range of emotions in such a short space of time: agony and misery, jubilation and happiness. Not that I was celebrating. I was never a great celebrator of goals anyway and certainly not now. I always felt the time to celebrate was at the end of a match, not while it was going on. I was more concerned about us getting back into our half of the pitch and shaping up properly with the back four and midfield firmly in place ready to start again. I was calling the other Arsenal players back for the remaining seconds because, unprepared, they could easily have done to us what we had just done to them.

But they didn't. Moments later it was all over, the end of one of the most bizarre matches I ever played in.

When you are playing in front of so many people, 100,000 vibrant, committed people, you see them as sort of cardboard cutouts, not as individuals. Only when we made our way up those steps to the royal box did I start to see people I knew, like a guy from Finsbury Park I recognised as an Arsenal fan. Fancy meeting you here? And only then did the occasion become real and personalised. Years later I was watching Arsenal play Chelsea in a big crowd and I think it was Aaron Ramsey who scored a goal and the place took off and I remember saying how I hadn't realised it was like this, all this noise and emotion. When you are playing you can never appreciate what it is to be a supporter in a big crowd.

Anyway, my mum and dad had come over from Ireland. My wife, Helen, and my in-laws were there and we all got stuck into the celebrations. We were staying at the Grosvenor Hotel and the atmosphere was altogether different from the year before when we were so down after losing to Ipswich when we had overwhelmingly been the favourites.

SAMMY NELSON

We didn't have a big squad, no more than 14 or 15 in those days, and they would be expected to play the vast majority of matches, including cup replays. There was only one substitute then and seasons were therefore gruelling; not like today when the big teams have 20 or 25 players at their disposal and there are far fewer fixtures.

I liked Terry Neill, our manager. I'm sure the Irish link helped, but he was a jovial, pleasant guy whose best signing was undoubtedly Don Howe. Don rejoined the club in 1977 and made such a difference as three domestic and one European final would indicate. Don was a great coach, a brilliant organiser who brought the best out of his players by respecting us as we respected him. Together, he and Terry made a great team. I think we would have won all four cups if everyone had been fit but the programme always counted against the successful clubs. In 1980 we lost to West Ham in the FA Cup and were the better team against Valencia in defeat. It was not unusual to play 70 games a season and often it was just too much. I remember once flying back from Europe on a Thursday and going up to Everton the next day for a match that night. It would never happen now.

I was lucky overall to have worked with so many good coaches in my time at Arsenal. They made me a better player. Don Howe was the coach when I first started, winning the Double in 1971, and then there was Ernie Whalley who was a tough taskmaster with us youngsters starting out in our careers. Ernie did not mess around and made sure you gave every match and every training session 100 per cent. Steve Burtenshaw was a good coach, too, and I can't forget Dave Sexton who was a top-class coach at Arsenal and Chelsea before going to Old Trafford. I would have been fortunate to have encountered any one of those, but to work with so many was very lucky.

Eventually, after so long at the club, I knew my time was coming to an end. Kenny Sansom was brought in to replace me and I was happy to move on in the knowledge that I had had a great time at Highbury. Brighton were in the First Division, somewhat surprisingly, but I played 50-odd games for them and was in the squad for the 83 final. Graham Pearce played at left-back for Brighton that day and I wasn't sorry not to be involved. I had played in all those finals and this was probably going to be Graham's only chance of a bit of glory.

I did a bit of coaching for a year at the end of my playing career but I never fancied management, uprooting a young family to go to the other end of the country, so in my mid-30s I trained to go into finance and thoroughly enjoyed my second career. I had a great time as a player and I will always remain an Arsenal supporter. I think I was fortunate to play for a great club with a huge history of achievement.

When the day came for me to leave for Brighton, Ken Friar, our secretary, said I was not to go until I had spoken to the chairman. Peter Hill-Wood left the City to come out to Highbury to say goodbye and wish me well, thanking me for my service. It was a classy act from a classy club. All the directors were like that, decent men who saw us players as individuals. Yes, I was very lucky.

PETER STOREY

Peter Storey
Defender/Midfielder
1962–1977

The only son of a carpenter, Peter Storey was born in Farnham, Surrey, in September 1945, five days after the end of the Second World War and VE Day. A well-built, talented England schoolboy footballer, he left formal education behind as a 15-year-old to join Arsenal in 1961, rejecting overtures from a number of clubs, including Tottenham, Chelsea and Southampton. He waited four years to make his debut in the First Division at Leicester City and went on to make more than 500 first-team appearances for the Gunners. A notable hard man, he featured in the Inter-Cities Fairs Cup Final triumph over Anderlecht in 1970 and went on to win 19 caps for England, making more international appearances than any of his Arsenal team-mates in the brilliant Double-winning team of 1970/71. As that side broke up, time took its toll on a body that went through the mill for the red-and-white cause and he bought a pub, strictly against the wishes of manager Bertie Mee. Storey became disillusioned with life at Highbury and joined Fulham in March 1977. His time at Craven Cottage was brief, however, and he called time on his career in November 1978, eventually retiring to live quietly off the beaten track in rural southern France with his fourth wife, Daniele, and a menagerie of animals.

Arsenal 2-2 Stoke City

FA Cup semi-final
Saturday, 27 March 1971
Hillsborough, Sheffield
Attendance: 55,000

Arsenal	Stoke City
Wilson	Banks
Rice	Skeels
McNab	Pejic
Storey	Greenhoff
McLintock	Smith
Simpson	Bloor
Armstrong	Mahoney
Graham	Bernard
Radford	Ritchie
Kennedy	Conroy
George	Burrows

Managers
Bertie Mee   Tony Waddington

Goals
Storey (2)   Smith
                          Ritchie

It was a standing joke in the Highbury dressing room that whenever I ventured over the halfway line, Don Howe broke out in a cold sweat, waving his arms on the touchline in the direction of our goalkeeper, Bob Wilson, and shouting: 'Get back, Peter, get back!' My strike rate from open play was a source of amusement and after one rare collector's item, a team-mate quipped: 'Snouty's scored ... quick, check if it's a leap year.' I was always 'Snouty' among the lads from my teenage years after interrupting a conversation among the senior professionals and being reprimanded by David Court to 'keep my snout out'.

I soon knew my place at Arsenal as a defensive enforcer too. Pure and simple, although I accept 'pure' might be pushing it a bit.

But I don't think anybody connected with the club, especially Don, our coach, was complaining on that sunny spring afternoon in Sheffield in 1971 when I scored twice against Gordon Banks, the best goalkeeper in the world.

Not only that, but my first was probably the finest goal of my career and the second, from the penalty spot in injury time, the most important.

At that stage of the season with another ten matches to play in the First Division, the FA Cup represented our best chance of success, especially after going out of the Inter-Cities Fairs Cup at the quarter-final stage four days earlier, on away goals to Cologne.

I had, in fact, scored in style to win the first leg 2-1 with a left-foot half-volley from the edge of the area, but I thought Cologne stunk the place out over there: first conning the referee into awarding them an early penalty and then spending the rest of the match rolling on the floor as if they had been shot whenever we tackled them.

There was a sense of bitterness, but we had no time to mope or feel sorry for ourselves on the flight home from West Germany with the semi-final against Stoke City at Hillsborough looming large.

There was an edge to the match because Tony Waddington's side had caned us 5-0 at the Victoria Ground in late September. We didn't carry mental scars from that heavy defeat, just a natural desire, as professionals, for revenge.

I remember Hillsborough was a picture as we ran out in our yellow-and-blue change kit, north London's finest fans filling the Kop and the Stoke supporters packed in at the other end.

We had arrived the hard way, drawn away in every round and needing a replay here and there to see off Yeovil Town, Portsmouth, Manchester City and Leicester City.

By contrast, one of the lads informed me on the coach going up that his paper said Stoke had been pulled out of the velvet bag first against Millwall, Huddersfield Town and Ipswich Town before being sent to Hull City in the last eight.

The Potters must have sensed their luck was in again midway through the first half.

I was well used to being described as the villain of the piece for my uncompromising approach, along with several unsavoury labels, such as 'the bastards' bastard', 'assassin' and 'thug'.

Now it occurred to me I might just be an unwitting villain for my part in Stoke's opening goal.

Harry Burrows curled over a corner from the right with his left foot, the ball fell and I whacked it away from the angle of the six-yard box, only to see my attempted clearance strike their centre-half Denis Smith and rebound freakishly into our net off the underside of the bar.

There was something funny going on at the other end too. Nine months earlier, England's undisputed number one Banks had made what many called the 'Save of the Century' during the World Cup in Mexico against Brazil, plunging to his right to flick Pele's downward header up and over the bar.

But here, as the Stoke skipper, he was a bundle of nerves and I thought it was only a matter of time before we took advantage and equalised. I might even have done so myself after Banks miskicked a free kick in his area, but my shot was blocked by a defender and the goalkeeper redeemed himself by turning John Radford's follow-up effort behind for a corner.

I could scarcely believe our misfortune when we conceded another goal on the half-hour, and the architect of our downfall on this occasion was equally surprising.

Charlie George's ability was never in question. Some of the things he did in training took your breath away and it bordered on the criminal that he went on to win just one England cap.

The danger appeared over when my mate Peter 'Stan' Simpson headed out a cross from the left by Burrows. Charlie chested the ball down and played a back pass to Bob Wilson. Unfortunately he did so without noticing that John Ritchie had stayed in the box, lurking behind 'Stan'. Ritchie seized possession in an instant, took the ball round Bob and slipped it into an unguarded net.

Don Howe and our manager, Bertie Mee, ensured the mood in our dressing room at half-time was serious rather than sombre. We didn't need reminding that the next goal would be critical. If we scored, and quickly, it was very much game on; if Stoke made it 3-0 in their all-white kit, it was very much game over.

In all honesty, it should have been 3-0. The second half was barely a minute old when Jimmy Greenhoff, their star £100,000 forward, slipped through a pass which had our skipper Frank McLintock floundering. John Mahoney was on it in a flash and clear, only to lose his composure when confronted by Bob Wilson, who smothered his shot.

The enormity of that moment became clear within 60 seconds. Geordie Armstrong's throw-in from deep on the left was hoisted high into the air over his own head by Ray Kennedy; two players went for the ball but it broke for me on the edge of the area. I wasn't renowned for my shooting ability but I took off and hammered the sweetest of right-foot volleys past Banks and a defender on the line.

Arsenal were back on the job but Stoke should have put us out of business. Greenhoff went clear from inside his own half on an electrifying burst but, with shades of Mahoney's miss, with the goal at his mercy his nerve failed him as the ball bobbled on the rock-hard surface and Greenhoff lashed his shot into the terracing on the Kop.

We kept pushing and pushing for the equaliser and the 90 minutes were up on the clock when Mike Pejic fouled George Graham. Geordie Armstrong floated in the free kick and there was an almighty scramble before the ball bounced behind for a corner off Banks.

I had never seen Gordon so ill at ease as that afternoon and, not for the first time, he argued furiously with the referee, Pat Partridge.

Despite being a World Cup winner and seasoned international of the highest calibre, the enormity of the domestic occasion for his club had clearly got to Gordon and the captaincy was a burden.

Over came Geordie's flag-kick; Banks was stranded and up went Frank McLintock for a header destined for the net, only for Mahoney to dive on the line and beat the ball away with his fist.

I've never been given to outward signs of emotion but I know my stomach tightened the moment Pat blew his whistle and pointed to the spot.

He'd had a perfect view of Mahoney's handling offence and Frank was busy now, celebrating and hugging the lads as if we were all off in the morning to get fitted for our FA Cup Final suits. Job done? I still had to execute and the consequences of failure didn't bear thinking about.

Football can be a lonely business when you lose, and it can also be a very isolating affair when the responsibility lies exclusively with you to beat the best shot-stopper on the planet from 12 yards.

George Graham said later that I must have lost half a stone taking that penalty – deathly quiet, just sweating, my shirt completely soaked.

The Big Match commentator Brian Moore had it right too when he said on telly: 'Storey is the man with the terrible responsibility and there are Arsenal players who daren't watch.' It was one of those defining moments I sensed would live with me for ever. Score and the goal would become almost a footnote, everyone's attention moving on to the replay. Miss and Arsenal were out of the FA Cup, it was all my fault and I'd never hear the end of it.

Charlie George was the only other penalty-taker in the team but he had gone off injured so the focus was exclusively on me.

I rarely made the headlines, not that it bothered me because my team-mates knew what I brought to the party, and when I did, I was often damned with faint praise.

So I wasn't surprised when the *Daily Telegraph* reported: 'With George off injured, Storey strode up to take the spot kick, not because of any deadball ability, but for his ice-cool temperament.'

I placed the ball down at the Leppings Lane end of the ground, blanking out the faces of Stoke fans contorted in hatred, walked back nine or ten paces, maybe betrayed a trace of nerves with a little skip and ran in to shoot.

It wasn't one of my most cleanly struck penalties but Banks blinked first, putting his weight on his right foot as if to dive in that direction; that gave me a split second to stroke the ball to his left – and into the net.

Gordon was distraught and complained: 'It wasn't even a good penalty. It wasn't far from my left but I couldn't react and get down.' I practised penalties every now and then in training at London Colney against Bob Wilson and Geoff Barnett, and scored time after time. The goal looked as big as anything then, but it was a very different story away from home in front of 40,000 fans wishing you to screw up. The goal shrinks and the opposing keeper looks like a giant. That's when you needed a technique to see you through.

I got the job of taking penalties by default. When Charlie wasn't around, no one else would touch them with a bargepole. Invariably, I used to settle the ball on the spot, brush my hands down my shirt or shorts, avoid eye contact with the goalkeeper, turn back and run up as if I meant business, concentrating with all my might before deciding at the last moment to shoot low inside one of the posts.

That penalty against Stoke went nowhere near the woodwork. I must have been worried about missing altogether.

I'd never call it fun, at times it was real pressure, and I was very lucky that the handful of penalties I missed in my career didn't count for much in the final analysis. Maybe I wasn't lucky; maybe I made my own luck.

Stoke's morale was shattered for the replay after blowing a two-goal lead, not to mention Mahoney and Greenhoff squandering clear chances to send them to Wembley.

We were supremely confident of meeting Bill Shankly's Liverpool in the final when the teams reconvened for a replay at Villa Park four days later. The only surprise is that we didn't manage more than two goals courtesy of George Graham's towering header and Ray Kennedy's tap-in.

Stoke's Mike Bernard had tried to stir things up earlier in the week, bragging that Charlie George had been in his pocket at Hillsborough. But the bravado merely served to rouse Charlie, who took an early opportunity to play an extravagant back pass to Bob Wilson, letting everyone know that he was not affected by his mistake on Saturday.

Now Arsenal's season was building to a crescendo, talk of the elusive Double growing with every league win.

All told, between 2 March and 20 April, there were nine victories in succession against Wolves, Crystal Palace, Blackpool, Chelsea, Coventry, Southampton, Nottingham Forest, Newcastle and Burnley. It's incredible to think Terry Paine, for Southampton at The Dell, was the only player to score against us in that run as we tracked down Leeds United at the top of the table and overhauled them.

No one had managed to do the Double since Tottenham's Glory Glory days a decade earlier.

Eventually, it all boiled down to two dramatic matches, two Arsenal matches which left me with very mixed feelings.

But before that, Stoke had their revenge of sorts, in our penultimate league match. I was caught by a late tackle which left me hobbling with damaged ankle ligaments. As I went off, Eddie Kelly came on and our brash young Scottish midfielder became an instant hero at Highbury with the only goal of the game.

Two days later Arsenal would be crowned champions of England providing we won at Tottenham or drew 0-0. Defeat or any kind of score draw and the title was bound for Leeds.

Some of our supporters were so desperate to be there they swapped their FA Cup Final tickets for a guaranteed seat at White Hart Lane.

As for me, I was the loneliest Arsenal player or fan in the stadium that night. I felt empty, totally out of it, after Ray Kennedy's late header proved decisive. I played in 40 of our 42 matches and of course I was desperate for Arsenal to win and take the title. And yet standing in our dressing room on crutches, I still felt something of a stranger. And I still felt like an outsider when our party burst into our local pub in Southgate shortly before midnight for a marathon five-hour boozing session.

Jimmy Greaves said he felt like a social outcast in 1966 because England didn't need him to win the World Cup.

Now I had a similar sensation.

I felt much worse, however, when Bertie Mee broke the news that I would be sitting on the bench alongside him and Don Howe at Wembley on the Saturday.

Bertie had been seduced by what Eddie Kelly could produce on the pitch and had clearly written me off because of the injury.

I was raging inside. After all, when our physio, Fred Street, asked the players if they had any strains, pains, bumps or bruises, he came to me and just said: 'Peter, any broken bones?' It took a hell of a lot to stop me playing and I wore that as a badge of honour.

Our relationship was never the same after Bertie subjected me to a fitness test so rigorous it could only have been designed to make me break down and ensure Eddie stayed in the team to face Liverpool.

I'm not a great believer in miracles but when I awoke early on Friday morning my ankle felt almost 100 per cent, all the pain had disappeared.

I arrived at Highbury for a spot of light training, informing the manager with a wide grin about the overnight transformation and that I was fit to play. Bertie's eyes narrowed as he told me: 'We'll soon see about that, Peter.' Several other members of staff could have supervised a routine fitness test, but Bertie took me on his own. He had been a skilled physiotherapist and tortured me. He drove me into the ground, my body was screaming for mercy but I refused to buckle.

Suddenly the agony was over, and Bertie just said tersely 'You'll do then', before turning on his heels and walking away.

So that's how I came to wear the yellow number four shirt at Wembley the following afternoon in furnace-like heat touching 90 degrees Fahrenheit – or 32 in today's money.

But the legacy of Bertie's brutal examination took its toll shortly after an hour. Socks rolled down, I had to make way for

Eddie. Maybe just as well, though, as he had the last touch to equalise before Charlie George's unforgettable winner.

When the final whistle sounded, I knew I would find it very difficult to forgive Bertie Mee and forget his callous treatment. I thought my loyalty deserved better.

That's why you will never find a photograph of me smiling as the other Arsenal lads celebrated with the FA Cup.

But I'll always have Sheffield.

PIERS MORGAN

I will never forget the moment I first fell in love with Arsenal. I was six years old when we won the FA Cup in 1971 and Charlie George, with his long hair flowing in the Wembley breeze, scored that 25-yard screamer against Liverpool.

Charlie lived out every Arsenal fan's dreams by going from being the guy watching from the North Bank to the striker that banged in the winner in the cup final and his poster went straight up on my bedroom wall alongside my other schoolboy heroes Bob Wilson and Frank McLintock, which must have been an annoyance to my dad as an avid Tottenham fan.

Dad went to every Spurs game for about 15 years when he was younger but he took his eye off the ball with me and, before he knew it, I was gone – I was with the enemy. Tottenham were so bad back then, having had their glory years in the 1960s, that Dad knew he was fighting a losing battle trying to convert me and even used to indulge me by taking me to games at Highbury.

My first live match was Arsenal against Manchester United at Highbury on 25 April 1972 when I was seven years old. We won 3-0, with goals from John Radford, Ray Kennedy and Peter Simpson. I still remember the thrill of it, the smell of the beer and everyone swirling around the packed terraces. I found it the most exhilarating thing in the world and was hooked straight away.

My eight-year-old daughter Elise is a big Arsenal fan. She has only been to one game and we were in the Diamond Club, dubbed on the club website as 'the finest place to watch football in ultra-exclusive luxury'. I said to her: 'You have no idea what the difference is between my first game and this.'

My media career has taken me all around the world but I have only missed one game either live at the stadium or on television in about 15 years as I always try to manage my work commitments around our fixture list.

Whenever I am in England, which is a lot more these days, I go to every home game and if I am at my second home in Los

Angeles I watch our matches on TV with a pal called Sean, a film scriptwriter who also happens to be the brother-in-law of the former British Prime Minister Gordon Brown. Midday kick-offs are always punishing because they are played at 4am local time.

Whatever I am doing I always try and watch the games and I once cut short a CNN interview with Mark Wahlberg, the Hollywood actor, on the day Thierry Henry made his comeback in the FA Cup against Leeds.

I asked Mark who his hero was and he named some guy from the Boston Red Sox. I said: 'Imagine if that guy was about to come back and pick up a bat in a real game!' He said: 'I get it.' So we stopped the interview and both sat and watched Thierry come on and score. Wahlberg was so excited for me, without having any idea who Thierry was, but he understood the analogy.

The two best players I have seen in my lifetime are Thierry and Dennis Bergkamp and trying to choose a favourite is like choosing your favourite child. I have always slightly leaned towards Bergkamp simply because, when he came in the mid-1990s, via the most unlikely route in Bruce Rioch, he transformed us in a way I don't think any other player has done. Thierry then came in and the pair of them were fantastic, but that Bergkamp signing was one of the greatest moments in Arsenal's history.

I also used to love Liam Brady when I was younger and was really sad when he left for Juventus, but I have had lots of favourites over the years. I went through a Malcolm Macdonald phase and loved Frank Stapleton and John Radford. George Armstrong was another who I had a big affinity with and 'Champagne' Charlie Nicholas was fantastic for a wonderful little period. I loved players like him who were a little bit different.

Ray Parlour is my cult hero because to me he is the personification of the club. I have got to know him really well and he is a lovely guy whose heart bleeds Arsenal. He just had that Arsenal never-say-die spirit, which has been so lacking in so many players in recent years, and he also loved a beer and a laugh.

He was my kind of footballer and also very underrated in my opinion and the truth is that in the last 15 years you can count the number of world-class players we have had on one hand. Pierre-Emerick Aubameyang is one, Mesut Ozil was one briefly before losing his way, Robin van Persie was one and Cesc Fabregas was one.

My favourite players were either the warriors like Patrick Vieira, Parlour, Lee Dixon, Nigel Winterburn, Tony Adams, David Seaman, Martin Keown and Steve Bould or the gifted ones: the Bergkamps, the Henrys, Brady or Robert Pires.

As well as having the privilege of watching some tremendous talents on the pitch during my Arsenal-supporting life, we have also been blessed with great managers. Arsene Wenger was fantastic for nine or ten years before he lost his magic. I maintain he should have left on a high after miraculously winning the FA Cup from 2-0 down against Hull City in 2014, but he kept chasing the dream and it was all rather sad the way it ended with fans arguing amongst themselves about 'Wenger-In' or 'Wenger-Out'. You all know what camp I was in.

As great as Wenger was, there is a good argument to say George Graham was just as good. He was only in charge for seven years but won two league titles and a European trophy, and went to Anfield and beat the best team in Europe to win the championship in 1989. I think George's record is underrated and often forgotten about when we talk about the best Arsenal bosses. He was very different to Wenger but what he achieved should not be underestimated.

Wenger made some great signings, not least Nicolas Anelka who was snapped up for a bargain £500,000 from Paris St Germain and sold for £22m to Real Madrid a couple of years later, but he inherited arguably the best back five in the world along with Dennis Bergkamp, and still had Ian Wright.

You could argue George Graham was just as transformative because he took over a club in the doldrums and brought the glory back. For me, that night at Anfield was the greatest of them all, even bigger than the Invincibles, because to go away from home and beat a team of that calibre by two clear goals was an incredible achievement, hence why they have subsequently made a film and a documentary about it.

I was 24 at the time and can remember every small detail about the match and have watched *Fever Pitch* many times. I have played golf with Alan Smith, one of the heroes of the evening, and I always tell him that group of players do themselves a disservice when they slightly play down their technical capabilities, because for that era, they were a fantastic team.

I watched that match with a group of junior doctors from Charing Cross Hospital in their apartment near Hammersmith. After the final whistle had blown, we raced to the pub half an hour before kicking-out time, and I just got as many pints down my neck as I possibly could. It was fantastic the way it all came together and the enormity of it all: the fact it was the end of a long wait to see my team win the league coupled with thinking we had blown it before Michael Thomas scored that goal right at the end. The Invincibles were fantastic but, for sheer drama, 1989 was the one for me.

I actually got fired as editor of the *Daily Mirror* the night before we became invincible, so it was the worst day of my career followed by one of the best days of my life. The next day all of the newspapers had pictures of me holding an inflatable Premier League trophy with a massive grin on my face on what should have been a miserable day. It was quite a funny juxtaposition.

I was there when we won the league at Old Trafford in 2002 and I was there when we won it at White Hart Lane in 2004 after throwing away a two-goal lead to draw 2-2 when Tottenham fans celebrated like it was their team who had been crowned champions. They were all going nuts and it was like, 'You do realise we have just won the league in your back yard. What is the matter with you?'

I was at the game with my dad, who is always very gracious about Arsenal's successes as he knows how much they mean to me, and after all the supporters had filtered away from the ground we were sat in the boardroom when Arsene Wenger and his assistant Pat Rice walked in. I swiftly brought the best bottle of wine I could find and we spent an hour celebrating: Wenger, Pat Rice, my dad and me. It was an amazing and surreal moment.

I have also had some memorable away days as an Arsenal supporter. I recall going to Florence to watch us play Fiorentina in the Champions League with my best friend, and as the players came out to warm up before the match they were right in front of us so I thought it would be a good idea to start singing 'There's only one Dennis Bergkamp' at the top of our lungs. Bergkamp looked up and gave us the thumbs up but, as I turned around, I saw hundreds of Fiorentina supporters all staring at us with murderous intent in their eyes and that is when I realised all the Arsenal fans were at the opposite end of the stadium behind a cage.

Arsenal won a penalty which Nwankwo Kanu missed, at which point 2,000 people stood up in unison to scream hysterical abuse at my mate and me. If he had scored, I think we would have been garrotted! That was one of the great moments but also one of the most reckless.

Another great moment was when I went with a Chelsea-supporting friend of mine to a game at Stamford Bridge in 1999. They had not beaten us for 18 matches and were 2-0 up with ten minutes to go when my mate tapped me on the leg and said: 'We have finally got you, you bastards.' Then Kanu scored what is to me the greatest hat-trick of all time, in the driving rain, culminating in the most absurd goal ever from the most impossible of angles. All us Arsenal fans left the ground singing 'Who needs Anelka when we have Kanu?' to the tune of 'Chim Cher-ee' from the Mary Poppins film.

We have had some fantastic moments at the Bridge: Sylvinho's screamer and Nigel Winterburn's long-range rocket. We always seemed to pull it out of the bag there, at least until Jose Mourinho arrived on the scene.

All the Manchester United games in the Wenger versus Alex Ferguson era were incredible: the pizza-gate game, the Ruud van Nistelrooy game. It was just two great teams and two great managers at their peak going at each other for eight years. It does not get any better than that and I really miss that incredible rivalry when we were possibly the two best club sides in the world with the two best managers. Those games were titanic and when I look back on it now, I think we were spoilt.

I spoke to Paul Scholes recently and he was full of praise for all those Arsenal teams, especially the one that won the Premier League and FA Cup Double in 1997/98. He is right that was an amazing team with Seaman in goal behind the famous back four, Vieira and Emmanuel Petit in midfield, Marc Overmars, Nicolas Anelka, Ian Wright and Dennis Bergkamp. It was a brilliantly organised team and you could make a very good argument that it was the best of all Wenger's title-winning sides.

I flew in from a Caribbean holiday for the game against Everton when we were confirmed as champions and Tony Adams scored the fourth goal with a fantastic volley; that was a magical afternoon.

France also won the World Cup that summer and I did a special edition of *The Mirror* in north London with the front-page headline 'Arsenal win the World Cup' with a picture of Vieira and Petit hugging each other after combining for the third goal in the final against Brazil. That was my finest hour as a newspaper editor and we even managed to get a few copies to Tottenham, Chelsea and West Ham just to cheer them up! The Gooners on my staff loved it, but the rest of them were spitting blood. There is a framed copy of that front page hanging in the press room of the Emirates, a fact I am very proud of.

If I had to put together my all-time favourite Arsenal XI it would be Seaman in goal, Ashley Cole at left-back and Tony Adams in the middle. I'd have to hold my nose and forget his past and have Sol Campbell in there too, with Lee Dixon completing my back four. Petit and Vieira would be easy selections as I think they are the best midfield pairing we ever had, with either Pires and Freddie Ljungberg or Pires and Liam Brady on the wings and Bergkamp and Henry up front.

I am pleased to say my four children are all Gooners and I go to matches with my sons, Albert, Spencer and Stanley. I sat them down when they were very young and had the same conversation with all four of them. I said: 'I have no problem if you want to support another team.' They all looked at me with their innocent little eyes and said: 'Really? You don't mind if we support Man United or Chelsea?' Then I would get serious and say: 'Of course not – as long as you don't mind if I never talk to you again in your life!' That is what my dad should have done, but thank God he didn't, because that would have been a pretty miserable existence.

Piers Morgan
June 2020